Openwork

Openwork
Poetry and Prose

ANDRÉ DU BOUCHET

SELECTED, TRANSLATED,

AND PRESENTED BY

PAUL AUSTER AND HOYT ROGERS

YALE UNIVERSITY PRESS ■ NEW HAVEN & LONDON

A MARGELLOS
WORLD REPUBLIC OF LETTERS BOOK

Frontispiece: Alberto Giacometti, *Portrait of André du Bouchet*, © 2014 Alberto Giacometti Estate/Licensed by VAGA and ARS, New York, NY.

Yale University Press books may be purchased in quantity for educational, business, or promotional use. For information, please e-mail sales.press@yale.edu (US office) or sales@yaleup.co.uk (UK office).

Set in Electra type by Tseng Information Systems, Inc.
Printed in the United States of America.

Library of Congress Cataloging-in-Publication Data
Du Bouchet, André, author.
[Works. Selections]
Openwork : poetry and prose / André du Bouchet ; selected, translated, and presented by Paul Auster and Hoyt Rogers.
pages cm. — (The Margellos world republic of letters)
Summary: "André du Bouchet, a great innovator of twentieth-century letters, has yet to be fully recognized by a wide circle of international readers. This inviting volume sets out to remedy the oversight, introducing a selection of du Bouchet's poetry and prose to English-language readers through the brilliant translations of Paul Auster and Hoyt Rogers. *Openwork* showcases pieces from the author's entire trajectory, beginning with little-known pieces from the 1950s, followed by major poems from the 1960s, and concluding with works written or rewritten in the poet's later decades. Throughout his life, du Bouchet devoted himself to long walks in his beloved French countryside, jotting down entries in notebooks as he rambled. These notebooks—more than one hundred all together—have emerged as signal works in their own right, and their musings are well represented in this anthology."—Provided by publisher.
Includes bibliographical references.
ISBN 978-0-300-19763-1 (hardback)
I. Auster, Paul, 1947– II. Rogers, Hoyt. III. Title.
PQ2664.U288A6 2014   848'.91409—dc23   2014014628

A catalogue record for this book is available from the British Library.

This paper meets the requirements of ANSI/NISO Z39.48–1992 (Permanence of Paper).

10 9 8 7 6 5 4 3 2 1

CONTENTS

ACKNOWLEDGMENTS

First and foremost, all of us involved in the creation of this book must thank Anne de Staël for kindly permitting us to reprint the work of her late husband, André du Bouchet. I would also like to acknowledge Cécile Margellos, Sarah Plimpton, John Taylor, Victor Martínez, Mary Ann Caws, and Clément Layet for their generous support of our project. In moments of doubt along the way, Michele Casagrande, Marco Genovesi, and José Francisco Hernández provided me with encouragement. I am grateful to Paul Auster, my friend of more than forty years, who collaborated with me closely on *Openwork*. His English versions of French poetry remain unsurpassed: in our quid pro quo about improving these translations, I profited far more than he. Helpfully, Siri Hustvedt took part in several of our discussions.

The various publishers of du Bouchet in France are listed in the Select Bibliography at the end of this volume. Though aware of the diverse conventions, we have consistently kept the first part of his surname in lower case. Many of the translations, as well as portions of the Introduction, have already appeared in *Poetry, AGNI, Plume, The Fortnightly Review,* and *Cerise Press.* Like the founders of the Margellos series, the editors of these journals deserve our sincere respect for sponsoring literature in translation. In addition, a number of our English versions were published in *The Random House Book of Twentieth-Century French Poetry* and *The Yale Anthology of Twentieth-Century French Poetry.* The second section of this book, *The Uninhabited,* originally appeared in a limited edition at Living Hand; Paul Auster has revised his translations especially for *Open-*

work. His literary agent, Carol Mann, ably seconded by Lydia Bly-
field, assisted us with the final stage of the proposal. We owe a debt
of thanks to John Donatich of Yale University Press, whose interest
in du Bouchet's work has brought this anthology to fruition. With-
out the precision of our manuscript editor, Laura Jones Dooley, and
the perseverance of Margellos WRL coordinator Elina Bloch, we
could never have surmounted the hurdles in our path. Attentive to
our wishes, Lindsey Voskowsky designed the cover.

Paul Auster and I dedicate this book to the memory of André du
Bouchet, who introduced us to each other in 1971.

—HR

The Restless Openwork
of André du Bouchet

> I know a wind in purpose strong—
> It spins *against* the way it drives.
> —Melville

An unjustly neglected giant of French literature—and obliquely, of several other literatures as well—André du Bouchet was one of the greatest innovators of twentieth-century letters. Trailblazing poet, maverick philosopher, multifarious critic, trenchant stylist, fearless anthologist, daring editor, prolific diarist, intrepid translator from three languages, tireless explorer of nature and the visual arts, he was an authentic iconoclast who has yet to receive his due, especially in the English-speaking world. This anomaly seems all the more inexplicable, given his dazzling renditions of Shakespeare, Joyce, and Faulkner into French, as well as his lifelong attachment to the classic authors of nineteenth-century America. A moving example of this is the epigraph from Melville quoted above, which du Bouchet placed at the head of one of his late works; and in most of his writings, the elliptical syntax and halting dashes of Dickinson inform every page.

Admittedly, du Bouchet's achievement far transcends all boundaries or allegiances, and the diversity of his ethnic background alone would make him a cosmopolitan figure, representative of our age of "translingualism" and immigration. In addition to his French versions of Anglophone writers, including authors as diverse as John

Donne, Gerard Manley Hopkins, and Laura Riding, he also enriched French literature with important translations from the German and Russian. All the same, affording du Bouchet the recognition he merits should be of particular concern to American readers, since his paternal family had ancestral ties to the United States, and he himself spent nearly eight years in New England at a formative stage of his development, befriending such key exponents of our poetry as James Merrill and Richard Wilbur.

By drawing the attention of the English-language public to du Bouchet's work, we hope this anthology will help to rectify a glaring omission. With remarkable far-sightedness, Paul Auster made the first step in that direction with his translations from the late 1960s and early 1970s (published in book form in 1976 under the title *The Uninhabited*). In my view, these translations of du Bouchet's poems from the sixties are still unequaled; somewhat emended by Auster, they are reprinted in the present collection. While later translators and omnibus anthologists of French verse have also tended to focus on his poetry from that decade, we have expanded the scope of *Openwork* to include pieces from the author's entire trajectory, both "poetry" and "prose." For du Bouchet, as for many French writers of the past two centuries, these modes of expression are intertwined and often indistinguishable.

While English-speakers have special reasons to become acquainted with this author's groundbreaking work, we are by no means alone in needing to catch up. Even in France—though du Bouchet was duly awarded the Critics' Prize of 1961, the Grand Prize of the French Academy in 1975, and the National Poetry Prize of 1983—the full import of his oeuvre is only beginning to make itself felt. With little regard for the self-promoting mainstream of belles-lettres, he frequently favored small presses and artists' editions, and many of his articles and essays in periodicals have yet to be collected. In verse, prose, and intermediate forms, he published more than seventy heterogeneous books in his lifetime, including twenty major translations from the

English, German, and Russian. Though highly respected among celebrated writers and artists, the friend of Paul Celan, Yves Bonnefoy, Louis-René des Forêts, Philippe Jaccottet, Jacques Dupin, Pierre Tal Coat, Alberto Giacometti, and many others, he maintained a cautious reserve toward the intellectual trends of Paris. As the epigraph from Melville implies, he was an inveterate contrarian. When Yves Bonnefoy introduced us in the autumn of 1970, du Bouchet wryly remarked: "With me you will learn to say no, no, no. Isn't that why you've come to France?"

A poet's poet in the tradition of Mallarmé, with a strong dose of the master's aloofness, du Bouchet never sought to attract a circle of younger disciples; nor did he try to advance his international reputation. According to his longtime American companion, Sarah Plimpton, though he returned to the United States briefly in 1970, he declined an interview with the *Paris Review,* which she had arranged through her brother, George Plimpton. With his son Gilles, du Bouchet made a trip to Crete (see the eponymous poem in this volume), and in his last years he attended several short conferences in Turkey, Eastern Europe, and Mexico, but he never took advantage of his early links to the English-speaking world. Throughout his life, he spent the greater part of his time in the French countryside, devoting himself to the long walks — first in Normandy and then in the Drôme — which nourished the creation of his notebooks. The entries were often jotted down during his rambles, especially during the decade of the fifties, and they have emerged as signal works in their own right. Once the entire corpus of these journals appears in print, the challenging texts he published in his middle and later periods will come into focus as trees fully integral to the understory below. In retrospect, more than a decade after his death, du Bouchet towers among his contemporaries with gathering insistence.

André du Bouchet was born in Paris in March 1924, the son of a physician, Nadia Wilter, and an engineer by training, Victor du

Bouchet. Though of Russian Jewish extraction, his mother had been raised in Paris; his father, of American and Russian parentage, had grown up in Odessa and then in Paris. In both these cities André du Bouchet's grandfather, Charles Winchester du Bouchet, conducted a distinguished medical practice. Born in Philadelphia, he was described by other family members as "very American"; his paternal ancestors had immigrated to the United States from France at the end of the eighteenth century and had intermarried with the local population of English descent. This American connection would prove decisive for André du Bouchet and his family during the crisis of World War II. Until then he and his younger sister, Hélène, enjoyed the comforts of bourgeois life in the Sixteenth Arrondissement, a well-to-do quarter of Paris. Given their multicultural relations, and the steady stream of maids, governesses, and au pairs who shared their apartment, they constantly heard many different tongues and dialects spoken around them. As du Bouchet later remarked: "I remember an entire childhood with foreign languages being murmured in the background." The children had plentiful access to books through their cultivated mother; her close friend, the novelist Nathalie Sarraute, lived in the same building.

This otherwise idyllic picture was overshadowed by the gloomy irascibility of the children's father, Victor du Bouchet, whose nervous fits were clinically diagnosed as schizophrenia in 1939. Throughout most of his life he remained unemployable. By 1940 André's mother, Nadia Wilter du Bouchet, was fully supporting the family, pursuing her medical career in a Norman village. Still an adolescent, the future writer bicycled to secondary school each day in the nearby town of Dreux, ten miles away. The worst blow of all came in May of that year, with the German invasion and the rapid collapse of France. About this cataclysm du Bouchet would later reminisce:

> I have a very exact memory of the moment when I realized
> people were fleeing on the roads . . . I felt that the world I'd

just discovered was caught up in a kind of rockslide. In June 1940, under the bombardments, we departed helter-skelter at first light . . . I recall quite well that I picked up a Greek dictionary, the Bailly, which was my only reading during the months that followed. It was a very violent experience: the world was destroyed. This was when I wrote for the first time, with the will to reestablish something, to attest to a connection I had barely glimpsed . . . before it was swept away.

Under the anti-Semitic laws of Vichy France, Nadia was no longer able to exercise her profession, and graver dangers loomed on the horizon. In December 1940, along with his parents and his sister, André crossed the Atlantic in the *Excalibur*, the last passenger ship to leave Lisbon.

After arriving in New York on December 6, 1940, the refugees made their way to Boston. There André's American grandfather temporarily took them in; but he could not afford to sustain them for long. He had led a prosperous life in Paris until 1939, but when the upheavals started in Europe he returned to the United States, his income reduced to a small pension. From this time forward the du Bouchet family was forced to split up. Far advanced in his illness, Victor was confined to a psychiatric institution. Since her diplomas were deemed unacceptable in the United States, at the age of forty-three Nadia was obliged to recommence her medical courses and lived in a student's room at a hospital. The two children were sent to boarding schools and later to college, always on a shoestring budget. For the spring semester of 1941 André obtained a place at the Loomis School in Windsor, Connecticut, expressly founded to provide aid to pupils in need. Thanks to his superior training in ancient Greek—and perhaps to the solace he had sought in the Bailly dictionary—he swiftly graduated from the classical course with honors.

In the autumn he entered Amherst College on the Harry de Forest Smith Scholarship for Greek, still in existence today. He received his BA summa cum laude in three years. Combining his two favorite disciplines, he wrote his senior thesis on "the influence of Cartesian philosophy on seventeenth-century literature." At Amherst he made friends with a fellow undergraduate, the poet James Merrill. Merrill would later recount to Paul Auster that he acknowledged du Bouchet as a genius even then, a prodigy whose gifts overawed him. Unfortunately, their college acquaintance was short-lived, since Merrill took leave in 1944 to serve as an infantryman in the US Army. That fall, at the age of twenty, du Bouchet began his master's degree at Harvard University on an Amherst stipend for graduate studies in English literature. In addition he received the Chapman Scholarship from Harvard, commemorating an alumnus who had died in France during World War I. Thanks to the funds from those two sources du Bouchet could forgo any major support from his hard-pressed mother.

Throughout his eight years in the United States André maintained a copious correspondence with Nadia, whom he rarely saw in person. It provides detailed information about his reading, his courses, his friends, and his extracurricular activities. He earned his MA at Harvard in English and by 1947 was a teaching fellow there in history and literature. In Cambridge, besides such French compatriots as the art historian Georges Duthuit, his younger colleague Pierre Schneider, and the artist André Masson, he frequented the poet and translator Richard Wilbur, who from 1945 was attending graduate school at Harvard on the GI Bill. Not surprisingly, given his troubled family background, du Bouchet underwent four years of psychoanalysis from 1944 to 1948. In November 1949, after his return to France, he would write in one of his notebooks: "Psychoanalysis has taught me my own limits: beyond them, it forces me to be free, and to weather the terrible squalls of reality."

The safety in which du Bouchet had spent the war years and their immediate aftermath could not make up for his sense of time lost in an involuntary exile, far from his native culture. As he wrote his mother in 1947: "This prolonged sojourn in America escapes the usual valuations: it's neither lovely nor dreadful. It has simply been a necessity for me to remain . . . a condition of my life. One more year to go. A sad year that means we know how to focus our efforts on true riches . . . Often I think of the celebration my return will be. I want to be equal to that." On the other hand he dreaded the "colères" (angers) of French society, still torn by the conflict between former "collaborateurs" and "résistants"; many of them harbored grudges about a wartime ordeal he had not directly shared with his compatriots. In August 1948, at the age of twenty-four, André du Bouchet regained the land of his birth. His mother had preceded him the previous year, continuing her medical career in Paris and placing his father once again in a psychiatric hospital. In 1949 du Bouchet married the future translator and anthropologist Tina Jolas, daughter of the American writer and critic Eugene Jolas, whose family he had met in New York. She had grown up in France and was also eager to resume her life there after the war. With her the poet would have two children: Paule, whose presence imbues her father's early notebooks; and Gilles, whose painting would later have an impact on his work.

On balance du Bouchet's experience in the United States had been neither wholly positive nor wholly negative; but for many facets of his oeuvre it would prove to be determinant. Despite the shattering of his family and the turmoil in Europe, he had continued his education, both formally and informally. His mastery of English was now complete: as he would later assert, it had become for him the academic language par excellence, the vehicle of argumentation and ideas. His separation from French had created in him a dual consciousness, a distance that encouraged him to approach his own language freshly, testing and stretching its possibilities as only an "outsider" can do. At a deeper level, he had entered the interstices where silence cohabits with speech. In a conversation less than a year before his death, he recalled that in this period English was the language in which he "didn't sputter," whereas French was the language of intimacy, "of everything that belonged to the order of muteness." After his long exile in America, he noted, French seemed "like a foreign language, inaccessible because too close."

Despite his youth, du Bouchet's work had already begun to appear in such leading US periodicals as *The New Republic*, *The Yale Quarterly*, and the *Partisan Review*. Now he gradually won access to journals of equivalent caliber in France. The most emblematic of these was the aptly named *transition*, a major cross-Atlantic forum in the postwar years, with a distinguished roster of American and European contributors. His older friend Georges Duthuit had just revived the publication, which had been founded before the war by Eugene Jolas; and on his arrival in Paris, du Bouchet served as an assistant editor for the review. He soon encountered Pierre Reverdy, whose poetry he had long admired; they became close friends and exchanged an avid correspondence. Du Bouchet published an incisive essay on Reverdy's work as well as studies of René Char and Francis Ponge, two more masters from the previous generation whom he befriended. Notably, he maintained his distances from the Surrealist movement, in accord with his preference for taut, understated imagery.

Despite his respect for his literary elders, he did not neglect his contemporaries. He forged close friendships with the artist Pierre Tal Coat and the poet Jacques Dupin; he soon met Yves Bonnefoy and Philippe Jaccottet as well, poets and translators who would follow his work with enthusiasm. Thanks to the intervention of Ponge, in 1951 du Bouchet published *Air*, a book of poems; in the same year he published his translation of *Knight's Gambit*, a set of short stories by William Faulkner. A second collection of verse, *Sans couvercle* (*Lidless*), followed in 1953, and he advanced his supranational concept of literature with self-assured essays on James Joyce and Boris Pasternak. In an anthology of Victor Hugo he edited in 1956, he displayed the kaleidoscopic method he would adopt toward his own literary production. By excerpting paragraphs and even short phrases from Hugo's poems and novels, he defied the conventional view of the author's oeuvre, stripping it of Romantic sentimentalism and inflated rhetoric. Admiringly, in his notebooks he cites Hugo's line "the earth is under words like a field under flies" as a pithy example of "words visualized."

As previously in the United States, du Bouchet availed himself of fellowships—research grants from the Centre National de Recherche Scientifique (National Center for Scientific Research)—to help finance his literary pursuits. The eminent philosophers Jean Wahl and Gaston Bachelard endorsed these disbursements, all the easier to obtain since du Bouchet was also working as a librarian for the center. The special fields of phenomenology and aesthetics, particularly as conceived by Martin Heidegger, would always form an essential undercurrent of his writing. Already in the early text « Les épines déchirantes » ("The piercing thorns . . .") of 1951, he had evoked the verse-form of Maurice Scève's *Délie* as "ten lines tight as a fist." In the three years from 1955 to 1957, he presented various studies of "poetic creation" to the oversight committee, honing in not only on Scève but on Hölderlin and Baudelaire. All the same, it eventually became apparent to all concerned that he had opted for poetry over poetics. Du Bouchet's fascination with what occurs in the gaps between the "dizains" of Scève would soon be reflected in the teeming blanks between his own verses. The late style of Hölderlin would also reemerge in his fragmentary syntax, uneven layout, and multivalent meanings. His fervent reading of Baudelaire culminated in the magisterial essay of 1956, "Baudelaire l'irrémédiable," comparable in heft to Bonnefoy's tribute to *Les fleurs du mal* a few years later. Baudelaire would always haunt both poets, seconded by Rimbaud and Mallarmé.

Tellingly, du Bouchet's final sketches for the CNRS projects already read like first drafts of his poetry. For example, he observes that

Baudelaire tried "to convert the future into a past," which could only result in "incompatibility." He ends his comments with the words:

> Baudelaire makes his sky of this incompatibility
>
> Incompatibility prime motor
>
> It is the sky of the annihilated image,
> the aura of the poem that expands and subsists
>
> from the vaporized image
>
> incompatibility wall in Baudelaire that will have served him as
>   a road

Clearly, this passage marks a transition to du Bouchet's mature manner, both in content and in technique — even down to the strikingly un-Baudelairian linkage of "motor," in all its senses, with "road." A "white motor" will soon figure strongly in his poems of this period, a metaphor both for the mechanics of movement and for the generative power of the sun.

In 1957 du Bouchet underwent one of the most painful crises of his life, his separation from Tina Jolas. The rupture arose from a double betrayal: her passionate affair with René Char, the younger writer's poetic mentor. For several years du Bouchet had a hard time regaining his inner balance; his readings, critical essays, and poetry served as helpmates toward stability. With a small notebook always at hand for spontaneous jottings, he continued his habit of extensive walks, especially near his mother's country house in the Véxin region of Normandy. As for Tina Jolas, she went on from a subsequent breakup with Char to become a noted ethnologist. Soon enough the tide would change in du Bouchet's favor. He attained a milestone in 1961 with the publication of *Dans la chaleur vacante* (*In the Vacant Heat*). This kinetic sequence of verse abounds in the gaping blanks, toppling metaphors, and syntactic twists which would characterize his middle and late periods. At the age of thirty-seven he now received widespread acclaim, garnering the Prix de la Critique, a national prize bestowed by literary critics. In his personal life he also arrived at an important turning point: getting over his divorce from Tina Jolas, he began a partnership with the American artist and poet Sarah Plimpton that would flourish for twenty years.

In 1966, along with Yves Bonnefoy, Louis-René des Forêts, Jacques Dupin, and Gaëton Picon, du Bouchet founded *L'Éphémère*, a legendary cultural review of wide-reaching influence, published by the Maeght Foundation. Two other renowned writers, Paul Celan and Michel Leiris, soon joined the editorial committee. The twenty numbers of the journal, the last of which was issued in 1973, provided a showcase for a broad range of topics, from literature to the visual arts, and from philosophy to anthropology. Texts from all periods of history appeared alongside each other: aesthetics prevailed over temporal contingencies. Here du Bouchet published his versions of Gerard Manley Hopkins, John Donne, and Laura Riding, as well as his collaborative translations of Paul Celan, Marina Tsvetaeva, and Ossip Mandelstam. Like Ezra Pound, he found such joint efforts useful in transposing a poem from one language to another. Above all, du Bouchet moved forward with his own poetry. After parts of the sequence had first come out in the review, in 1968 he published his collection *OU LE SOLEIL*; he left the title in capitals, so that the first word hovered between "or" and "where"—though the initial verse began with the phrase "où le soleil" (where the sun).

In 1971 du Bouchet acquired a house in the isolated village of Truinas, surrounded by the mountains of the Drôme. His constant wanderings in this region, one of the best-preserved natural areas in France, colored his notebooks for the rest of his life. But his preoccupation with art also came to the fore: in 1972 he took up his earlier compositions on Giacometti, expanding them into the full-length book *Qui n'est pas tourné vers nous* (*Which Is Not Turned Toward*

Us). The leading authority on his work, Clément Layet, has observed that from this time forward, his creative methods resembled those of the visual arts: "In reshaping his textual materials, sometimes written twenty years earlier, as though he were digging at or adding to their substance, André du Bouchet's writing approached sculpture more and more closely. His working tools were pages, a typewriter, scissors, glue, and a drawing board, where the thumb-tacked sheets evolved according to his successive looks of appraisal." The author himself commented that he proceeded "sometimes by cutting, sometimes by development. When it's a matter of what we might call 'prose,' it's mostly through a development which entails more cutting in turn, by a movement of drift within repetition. For poems, it's more like pulverizing, condensing." During one of our earliest discussions in 1971, he also stressed the need for a lengthy period of gestation: "Leave what you write in a drawer for a couple of months or a couple of years, even a couple of decades," he told me. "Later you'll find out why these words came to you, and where to take them from there."

Du Bouchet had always used his notebooks as an ore from which to extract subsequent texts; but increasingly, even his printed writings would undergo later revisions—often thoroughgoing—that would require further publications. In 1979 he reworked many of his contributions to *L'Éphémère*, weaving them into the complex fabric of *L'incohérence* (*Incoherence*). Though the changes were profound, such shifts may seem common enough when revamping pieces from periodicals. But in the case of du Bouchet, the recycling could apply to entire volumes that had already appeared, segments of which would migrate from one opus to another. The technique might be compared to the transfer of a draftsman's sketch to other media while conserving either the broad outlines or certain details of the preliminary drawing.

The author's engagement with the visual arts would in fact lead him to present many of his books as inner colloquies with painters and engravers, accompanied by their images. Along these lines, the most catalytic of his silent partners were Pierre Tal Coat, Jean Hélion,

Alberto Giacometti, Bram van Velde, Geneviève Asse, and Miklos Bokor. And in an especially moving gesture, coming from such a private poet, the vast meditation of 1984 entitled *Peinture (Painting)* takes the artworks of his son, Gilles du Bouchet, as its point of departure. From the late seventies onward, this personal link with painting was further strengthened by the writer's relationship with Anne de Staël—the daughter of Nicolas de Staël and herself an artist—who gave birth to his third child, Marie, in 1976.

In a reflex similar to his dialogue with the visual arts, du Bouchet adapted translation to his desire to stretch the envelope of literature. His French versions of works written in other languages, chiefly the ones from the German and Russian, have been criticized—wrongheadedly—for a few minor semantic shifts. No doubt English was his most accomplished language after French; with the other two, as I have already noted, he had to rely on assistance. His incisive renditions of Shakespeare alone—of *Pericles* and *The Tempest*, for example—would have earned him a lasting place in the annals of literary translation. But even in the case of English, slavish exactitude was not the essential point. Whereas conventional translation starts with a source language and aims at a target language, for du Bouchet both source and target lay elsewhere: in the unspoken, at the threshold where poetry begins to form. His quest for the fundamental language underlying translation runs parallel to the theories of Walter Benjamin. Just as du Bouchet perforated the walls of literature and art to reveal the unexplored spaces they share, in his recastings of German, Russian, and English he subtly pierced the divisions between languages. After all, in his childhood, many linguistic voices had overlapped, including those of Latin and Greek; and when he returned from America, French itself had become like a foreign tongue to him. Astutely, he recognized this not as a hindrance but as an opportunity. His seminal meditation of 1986, "Notes sur la traduction" ("Notes on Translation"), leaves off with the words: "French. I still have to translate from French. We do not realize: that has not been translated."

In the final decade of his life, from 1991 to 2001, du Bouchet crafted new poems in a never-ending stream. But coevally, he summed up his own achievement as a writer, with a lucidity rarely rivaled in literary history. He carried out this reprise on two seemingly opposite fronts. On the more obvious level, he orchestrated his past texts—from the earliest to the latest—into comprehensive ensembles, which alter and expand his existing books. For example, in the volume *Alberto Giacometti, « Dessin »* (*Alberto Giacometti, "Drawing"*) of 1991, he crystallized his decades of thought about the single artist who had most influenced his writing. Along the same lines, he issued three successive "anthologies" of his work—in the supple definition we must apply in his case, which is highly sui generis. The series began in 1995 with the deceptively neutral title *Poèmes et proses:* a set of revised older pieces and new additions. But after he was diagnosed with leukemia in 1996, du Bouchet seems to have hastened the recapitulation of his oeuvre. The second selection, *L'ajour* (*Openwork*), of 1998, was followed in 2000, only a year before the author's death, by a third: *L'emportement du muet* (*The Mute's Outrage*). In contrasting ways, both titles illuminate the central axes of his lifework: the open-ended dynamism of change and the seething silence that underlies speech. Through ceaseless experiments, he had learned to use his early exile to the advantage of his quest. His disjunction from his language and culture had allowed him to arrive at a form of expression beyond the accidents of time and place. He had mastered a prose style that hybridized the visual and literary arts, an approach to translation that heightened its textual flexibility, and a free-floating poetry that overstepped the conventional bounds of language.

The other channel taken by this final burst of creation was equally momentous, though it appeared unobtrusive on the surface. In 1989, du Bouchet permitted the literary critic Michel Collot to publish a selection of passages from the journals he had maintained over the decades, under the anodyne rubric *Carnets, 1952–1956* (*Notebooks, 1952–1956*). In his afterword, Collot explained that he had drawn on sixty of the pocket-size sheaves the poet habitually took with him on his excursions. As I have already mentioned, these often furnished the nucleus for published writings. But until his encounter with Collot, it had never occurred to du Bouchet to print verbatim the raw materials of his work, his spontaneous jottings in the field. Collot rightly thought they would shed a clarifying light on his oeuvre; and thanks to the impetus given by his friend, du Bouchet began to unlock his workshop for his readers, inviting them to look over his shoulder. In a long entry published only recently, he greeted Collot's intervention as follows:

> . . . the choice given by Michel Collot — without whom these
> pages
> would not have existed   — a choice where I counted
> for nothing — I return them
> today to an existence : to what may have a power of appeal.

But then the poet began to reassume his authorial control, positioning these snippets from the past on his drawing board. With himself as sole editor, he issued *Carnet* in 1994, widening the earlier collection to span the years 1950–1961. In that volume he continued to head the selected entries with month and year, as Collot had done; but already in *Carnet 2*, published in 1998, which covers 1962–1983, he suppressed the months and divided the sections only by the year of their composition. By the time he reached *Carnet 3*, which appeared in 2000, he had reduced the word "notebook" to a subtitle, pointedly calling the work *Annotations sur l'espace non datées* (*Undated Annotations on Space*). There could be no clearer demonstration of du Bouchet's resistance to the concept of chronological order, as well as his impulse to invent new genres out of preexisting literary modes. As Antoine Emaz has observed, the author's switch from Collot's plural "notebooks" to the singular "notebook" affirms the primacy of the form itself over "the concrete supports of writing." In the *Annotations*, it is as though "the notebook had passed from the status of a rough draft, the genesis of a parallel poetic work, to that of an autonomous poetic work, with no relation to any historically adjacent publication."

In what may have been his last poem, du Bouchet paid tribute to a renowned fellow poet, Louis-René des Forêts. Returning to the more emotive style of his early verse, he virtually wrote his own epitaph:

> A man walks on the shoreline of language, a child at first; and then, moving from page to page, he arrives at a great age from which it would seem that only an instant, or several instants, had divided him.

> man   child   nothing

> a child goes to the man in the air . . .

We should recall that du Bouchet's first book was entitled *Air*; and in an early undated poem that came to light only recently, he addresses poetry as the "diamond of breath." The link with the "air" of words could not be clearer, just at the point when they fall silent. In all these instances, as in the notebooks, du Bouchet reveals an intimate side often hidden in the published works of his middle and late periods. As it happens, the homage to his friend adverts to a crucial moment that decided the fate of the "cahiers" themselves.

Anne de Staël, whom du Bouchet married in 1999, has recounted the incident. In December 2000, at their house in Truinas, he amassed all his notebooks with the firm intent of burning them; he wanted to destroy every page without leaving a trace. Having already extracted three volumes of passages from these "cahiers," in addition to the one prepared by Collot, he feared that after his death more excerpts would be needlessly divulged. But just as he was about to carry out his resolve the telephone rang, stopping him in his tracks. The wife of Louis-René des Forêts had called to tell du Bouchet that her husband had died. "Then we are all dead!" du Bouchet exclaimed.

Forthwith he abandoned his plan once and for all. The poet's gesture suggests an acceptance that he, like all authors, must ultimately yield to those who will go on living. Readers, critics, and editors will make their own choices about which texts seem most salient to them, and their judgments will shift over time with the historical evolution of taste.

If du Bouchet composed his own epitaph in the poem I have quoted, I should also cite one more: it reflects the other side of the coin, the austere self-abnegation of his late work. Heedless of his delicate state of health, in 2001 the poet insisted on going to Truinas in the dead of winter to witness the snowfalls there, so often evoked in his writings. The doctors had given him several more years, but by March he underwent a massive relapse of leukemia. He received his final publication, a set of new poems called *Tumulte*, in his hospital room. As always, the title of the book said everything: the turbulence of his restless energy, the letters and blanks whirling like a blizzard on the page, the never-ending tumble of universal forces. One of the poems in that last collection, "A l'arrêt" ("At a Standstill"), reminds us that du Bouchet was not a poet who led a purely verbal existence, only through the medium of words: he lived in them, but he also lived "outside" them. As the poem repeatedly declares: what is important is "dehors"—what is "outside" our grasp. A supreme example of his openwork, the term implies thousands of meanings at once: being "outdoors" in the shifting phenomena of nature but also being "outside" the limits of language, "outside" the constraints of human consciousness, and "outside" existence itself:

but

outside
without having

stopped it

I cannot

André du Bouchet died on April 19, 2001, and was buried in Truinas.

If I have stressed du Bouchet's American years in this brief biography, it is for two reasons. In the first place, that little-known part of his history may bring him closer to the English-speaking readership. But far more significantly, I believe the period of his escape from France and exile in the United States exercised a lasting influence on his work. In those eight years, starting when he was barely sixteen, he went through a tidal wave of shocks: the collapse of France, the invasion by the Germans, the anti-Semitic persecution of the Vichy regime, the hasty flight to Lisbon, the crossing to New York, the inability of his grandfather to provide a haven in Boston, the permanent unraveling of his family, the forced adjustment to boarding school, the separation from his mother, the rejection of her professional degrees, the irredeemable madness of his father, the uneasy disjunction from European suffering—and above all, for such a literary youth, the abrupt plunge into another language for both intellectual and everyday use. The self-effacement of du Bouchet's poems does not mask the difficult experiences behind them, which continued into his adulthood. For example, his betrayal by both Tina Jolas and René Char was a heavy blow; in one of his journal entries around this time, he fears his family will "blow apart"—but he could have written, "blow apart again." And then at the end of his life there was the lingering leukemia, which he faced with stoic resignation.

At a crucial stage of du Bouchet's development as a writer, French began to seem like a foreign idiom to him. On top of the multiple ethnic and linguistic strains (in both senses of the word) he had already inherited, he now became to some degree a migrant within his own country of origin. His transpositions from one language to another, or from one art to another — such as his fusion of painting with literature — were never acts performed within the comfort of an aesthetic "homeland." Instead, they represent a perpetual motion: cultural and verbal fragments rise and converge only to shatter all over again, in a tireless motion forward. This internalization of exile might explain why he was never tempted to live abroad again and why he rarely traveled for extended periods outside of France. It was as if his lengthy stay in the United States had exhausted his tolerance for daily life in other cultures. On the other hand, since he subsumed various nationalities within himself, he had no need to cultivate their outer trappings. His childhood and adolescence had unfolded against a backdrop of linguistic pluralism, and he embodied it no matter where he lived; he maintained that polyvalence through his translations and foreign friends. His twenty years with Sarah Plimpton, who spoke little French when he first met her in Paris, were somewhat like sharing an outpost of America in France — in a contrary movement to that of his youth.

Given the intricacy of du Bouchet's origins and influences, it is hardly surprising that his literary output is dauntingly complex. In putting together our reader of his work, Paul Auster and I have tried to give a balanced glimpse of the author's vast creation, and we have felt justified in proceeding with a free hand. Du Bouchet himself allowed Collot to select entries from his journals as he saw fit, lending an even greater elasticity to his oeuvre. By so doing he acknowledged the right of a conscientious reader to exercise his or her own control over his writings, and even to countermand authorial dictates. In other words, he might be said to have endowed future editors with an ongoing permission to devise an André du Bouchet of their own, just as he had done with Victor Hugo. The ultimate stage of his "openwork" would be to devolve it to the imaginations of others.

At the time of his death du Bouchet had already given his intellec-
tual heir, the philosopher Clément Layet, license to carry out such
a project. The result, the Seghers volume of 2002, combines Layet's
lengthy exegesis of four du Bouchet texts with a selection that aban-
dons all chronology, excerpting passages from various works in "verse"
and "prose," just as the author himself had done when regrouping his
previous compositions. I should add that the leeway with his words du
Bouchet granted to others had always impressed me. As I transposed
his poems at various points from 1970 to 2000, I noticed that while
he kindly answered questions, he preferred to leave his translators a
wide margin of freedom. His only explicit suggestion — for the ending
of "Célérité" ("Swiftness") — was actually a distinct departure from
the original (see Part Three of our anthology). His liberality seemed
all the more striking, given his multilayered fluency in casual as well
as formal English, dating back to his long American sojourn.

In our collection, as in many reeditions sanctioned by the author
in his lifetime, the blank spaces have been slightly compressed to
accommodate a new book size and format. In works left as manu-
scripts, such as the notebooks, we often have no exact indication of
his wishes, and so we must improvise in any case. Thanks to du Bou-
chet's final act of selflessness in preserving them, we still possess such
invaluable passages as the early entry about a voyage from Venice
to Greece, included here. Clément Layet published that sequence
only recently, along with many other notations by du Bouchet, in the
spring of 2011. We hope that all of them will appear one day, perhaps
in facsimile, and that du Bouchet's letters will be printed as well. The
letters to his mother in the American years, like his exchanges with
artists and writers in his maturity, are fascinating not only as autobiog-
raphy but as documents of an era.

Up till now, in the omnibus translations of modern French verse,
du Bouchet's poems may have seemed baffling to many readers,
through no fault of the editors: lacking space, these compendia must
showcase each author's most characteristic traits. Thanks to a wider

compass we can begin to trace how du Bouchet's mature style evolves from its origins. The early poems and notebook entries disclose that his innovations flow naturally from the tradition of Baudelaire and Rimbaud—even Hugo, whom he boldly spliced in his anthology—after passing through the prism of his immediate mentors such as Reverdy and Char. All these ancestors loom large in du Bouchet's writings from the forties and early fifties, which echo the sonorous music, emphatic metaphors, and synesthesia of his predecessors. From these beginnings he gradually modulates to the more reserved tone and Mallarméan spacing of the poems Paul Auster first transposed. But in his final phase, by far the longest of the three, instead of repeating his "trademark" manner, as a lesser poet or artist might have done, du Bouchet leaps beyond his own maturity, fracturing its hard-won molds into ever more daring and disintegrated forms. Unlike his midlife achievement, his early and late production remains virtually untranslated, to the impoverishment of world literature in English.

Respecting the schema outlined above, we have organized our reader in three parts; but given du Bouchet's penchant for constant recycling, our selections cannot—and should not—obey any strict chronology. Instead, they coexist in an interchange with one another across the decades: the poem "Je ne vois presque rien" ("I See Almost Nothing"), for example, from du Bouchet's earliest period, is printed here in his revised version of 1995. Even so, our initial sequence consists of little-known pieces from the 1950s; the middle section offers the major poems of the following decade; and the closing segment is composed of works written or rewritten in the poet's later phase. Both the first and third portions are made up mainly of writings that have never appeared in English before. As I have observed, the lifeblood of du Bouchet's oeuvre courses through his notebooks, of which he left more than a hundred. His approval of Collot's edition, his own volumes of published excerpts, and his final decision to preserve the originals intact, all serve to legitimize them as integral to his writing. They have not been neglected in this anthology, especially the entries of his formative years; and the last poem in our selection was entitled by du Bouchet "From a Notebook." As his own reuse of these extemporaneous texts affirms, they illuminate and complete his life-work, revealing its coherence as a lucid sierra *as well as* a far horizon of mist-shrouded peaks.

Some book titles are fairly neutral or refer only to one of many aspects of a book; but du Bouchet's headings always wield an intentional heft—even more so when they seem noncommittal. By lending a special weight to the title of our anthology, we mean to imitate his practice. The heading *Openwork* was inspired by *L'ajour*, the title he gave to a set of excerpts from his oeuvre in 1998, several years before his death; otherwise, our selection bears no resemblance to that compilation at all. The French and English words often turn up as dictionary stopgaps for each other; but as always, no neat equivalence pertains. Every translation implies an option, a slant—and ultimately, a stance. "Ajour" resonates with many echoes in French: phrases we could render as "to light," "day by day," or "up to date." At every level du Bouchet's writings are flooded with light, graphically portrayed by the blanks that dominate his pages. Like the spatial demarcations in a painting, they bring out the full force of each word, each "object of thought." From a related perspective, his work feeds on the cycles of the sun from dawn to dusk, the "white motor" of the eponymous sequence included here; and *L'ajour* begins with a piece called "un jour de plus augmenté d'un jour" ("One More Day Increased by a Day"). Then, too, du Bouchet's whole collection under that heading not only revisits but also revamps earlier texts that stretch back as far as 1972, "bringing them up to date." Here revision must be understood in a more literal sense: not as an improvement but as a recasting "in the light of" the present moment. To hear another reverberation: "ajournement"—like the English "adjournment"—tells us that this day's session has ended, but also implies that it will be followed by another, at some point in the future. Du

Bouchet had used this very word as the title of a previous book, with all the accompanying overtones.

By settling for the helpmeet "openwork," English must jettison some of the French allusions to light, day, revision, and adjournment. But as often happens in the process of translation, something is gained as well as lost, the goal being to keep the black column balanced with the red. Like "ajour" the English word refers to artifacts that consist of holes as much as solids, whether embroideries, paper cutouts, filigrees, or retraced drawings and etchings like Giacometti's—not coincidentally, the artist about whom du Bouchet wrote most often and whose techniques he adapted to writing. In a sense such works are absent as well as present, a way of positing nothing and everything at once. The analogy with du Bouchet's own blank-pierced lines is self-evident, but here is where the English "openwork" compensates for the missing connotations of the French "ajour." As the term seems to suggest, the interstices in such an opus turn it into a "non finito," a refusal to reach any conclusion. It hovers in a perpetual state of flux, of receptiveness to the word and to the world. Like the air in an openwork sculpture, both are temporarily captured by the verbal net but freely pass through it. And yet the wholeness of those wider spheres—of language, of reality—can be surmised in each of the poem's interlocking voids.

As I have pointed out, du Bouchet often excavated fragments from his notebooks to reuse them in his published poems and prose. In earlier collections such as *Air* and *Dans la chaleur vacante*—titles that both suggest a kind of "openwork"—he seems to have striven for finished versions, in accord with common praxis. But in his later phase he reshapes his already printed works, often changing them radically. The parsing of these metamorphoses could easily spawn a shelf-load of dissertations. But the basic principle is clear: for du Bouchet, transformation is writing itself. Not only does *L'ajour* present multiple shifts in preexisting texts, it even alters selections from the preceding anthology, *Poèmes et proses*, published just three years before. This renders the notion of an "état définitif" (definitive state), even when applied by the author himself on occasion, more than a little suspect. Probably he would have approved the ironic turn: "definitive—for now." As in lithography, "état" (state) might denote a stage equally valid with the others in a series. For that reason the seeming volatility of du Bouchet's writing should not deceive us; his oeuvre evinces a thoroughgoing unity. In fact, it can only be understood by taking it as a whole; but by the same token, each of its parts reveals its totality, like every coded cell of an organism.

All the same, is a du Bouchet "anthology" even possible? By setting the word in quotation marks, I am admitting the intrinsic danger of sticking samples of his massive geology into a small box, especially since the strata continue to upend as his notebooks rise to the surface. But I would maintain that any sample of his words furnishes a valid illustration of his fundamental method. Reflections of his readings, of artworks he has examined, and above all of his rambles in the countryside, his journals ripple with a keen sensibility. Even in his more standard publications, instead of devising set pieces to place on display, as a goldsmith might, he provides us with cross-sections of the ore itself. The poetry and prose emerge from the notebooks, to be melted down in turn and recast later on. All are only proposed as a brief view of the mountain, most of which remains invisible: like every lifework, every poem or essay, every metaphor—even every word. When du Bouchet was embarking on the mature phase of his oeuvre, he observed: "Poetry without any padding would be poetry with big gaps—it would be riddled with gaps." As he moved into his later period these gaps became wider and wider, and readers were obliged to make some strenuous leaps.

Strenuous, but not prohibitive: especially in the final reaches of his work, du Bouchet was pursuing the techniques of visual artists. If we compare the notebook entries (pp. 72–77 in this anthology) that gave rise to "Le voyage" of 1956 with the poem itself, we can observe how the original metaphors were progressively fractured, overlaid, and recombined. By the time they reach their later avatar as "Sur le pas," the bare, aerated version of *Dans la chaleur vacante* (1961), they have become both more streamlined and more multivalent. Like Giacometti in his sculptures, du Bouchet has refined his initial images to a level where they almost seem effaced; but paradoxically, they have also attained an intense "thereness," a concentrated presence. An even more radical distillation occurs in the late poems: as an example, take the multiple shifts from the early "state" of the poem "Je ne vois presque rien" to its last known revision in 1995 (included in our selection). As in the final paintings of Willem de Kooning, the late works of du Bouchet contain large stretches of white canvas that force the remaining forms to stand out with breathtaking purity.

When we consider du Bouchet's recurring keywords and tropes, we are tempted to cite the evolving leitmotifs of a musical score; and as his notebooks reveal, he was a devotee of classical music. Paul Auster has reminisced about how he often listened to records with the author in the early seventies, at his apartment in the Rue des Grands-Augustins. In the same period du Bouchet and I would frequently set out from there, cross the Pont Saint-André des Arts, and visit the Louvre: his aperçus on Sumerian sculpture, Delacroix, and Patinir are still vivid in my memory. He was always at pains to point out the importance of the single contour, the single brushstroke, the single color transition — with that same focus on the primacy of the fragment that informs his poetry. But again, the techniques of modern art afford the closest parallel to his work. De Kooning devised many of the black-and-white paintings of his first major exhibition in 1948 by tracing definite figures, then painting over them repeatedly until they appeared almost unrecognizable. Yet even in later abstractions like the hugely colorful oils of the 1970s, an occasional object such as a woman's red shoe leaps into view. The constant overlap of foreground and background, the intricate slippage of half-glimpsed outlines into each other, the dizzying modulations of thickness and texture — all correspond to similar traits in du Bouchet's writings. However abstract they may seem, they are always bonded to the immediate and the concrete. The underlying sensory impressions still resonate, if only as "force fields" that fuel the text's coexistent meanings. As de Kooning said: "Even abstract shapes must have a likeness."

In his Séghers essay on four of du Bouchet's poems, Clément Layet has demonstrated the endless weft of ideas each of them contains. His analysis is philosophical, and it undoubtedly holds true; yet I would also suggest a more basic approach, anchored in the senses. Du Bouchet, an avid walker and motorcyclist, never lost his passion for the countryside, particularly as it shuffles through the ceaseless nuances of the weather. In a poem like "Cession" ("Giving Over"), included here, he starts simply with the wind, the summer dryness, and the sundown narrowing the sky. In that clarity, the folds of the terrain stand out. Over time, our successive breaths strip us of being as surely as the wind scours the fields; but that rhythm is also the source of our life. An equipoise is reached in the middle lines, where the sky is both wall and light—like our forehead, a surface that harbors depth. From that stasis, the blue air of infinity impels us forward. The word "foot" is used as a stable marker, but it implies the act of walking. The "gathering anew" (in French, "se recomposer") of the poet is also the composition of his "verse" (derived from the Latin for "turning the plow"), alluded to here by the furrowed field. On manifold levels, "nothing quenches his step."

Du Bouchet always grounds his work in primal sensation; but the interplay between reality and trope is never simplistic. As he scoffed in one of his interviews: "People think I spent my life in front of a mountain—but in fact, it isn't so! I never spoke about mountains more than when I wrote *Dans la chaleur vacante,* but there weren't any around. If I settled down later across from a mountain in Truinas, it's because I felt an attraction . . . ." But was that symbolic mountain of the poems any more intangible than the later mountain of stone and ice? Even if we touch a mountain, we are only laying our hand on a small patch of rock. From afar, we think we survey the mountain in its totality. But what of the mountain at night, or hidden by fog? We cannot see it, but we know it is there. Or do we? The fact is that we never encompass a whole mountain from any vantage point. Even from high above, we cannot observe the core of the rock below its many surfaces. In a horizontal view, we register only one of the mountain's many faces. All of these vary as well, according to the vagaries of lighting and weather or the play of shadows made by clouds. Such effects are beautifully limned in a sentence from "Le voyage," which I would translate as follows: "But the white rock-face—gilded and glazed by the light that picks it out and sweeps it with dim mountains." Du Bouchet was a translator of Gerard Manley Hopkins, and he twists the familiar phrase "the mind has mountains" inside out. Not only does he internalize the landscape, he externalizes the mindscape. Even in nature, the mountain we can see is always a metonym. That is why it is so much like a word: never the thing or the concept itself, words only point in their direction, before relapsing into their own inscrutability.

This semantic seesaw becomes even more manifest when du Bouchet sets us before a painting, as in "Peinture," the first poem by that title in our reader. Art, like poetry, swings subtly between the palpable and the ineffable. In the canvas held up to our view, the objects depicted wait for us to notice them. We might assume that they are only a simulacrum. But since reality is filtered by the mind, it is always a resemblance, and so resemblance "is itself reality." But with this nuance: in art, we cannot possess what it offers us. That is why its surfaces can bloom, in pure, unattainable desire—as a halo, an effulgence that pierces mere appearance. Branches, a doorway, or a tile grant us an emotion that is "almost unmoved." "Almost," because we are stirred by a deeper awareness: this gift we have received from art (or poetry), this paradox of repetition and freshness, is in fact our only access to the world. What we longed for was but a seed of infinite expansion; thanks to art (or poetry), it opens and flowers. The end of the poem circles back to its beginning. The objects of external reality also wait for us to notice them. On both sides of the looking glass, they unveil their endless ambiguity. The unseen blue of the sky, reflected by the window, is inseparable from the window itself. As we pause expectantly, what seemed so recognizable at first takes on another name — or none at all — and in our watchfulness . . . it has already flowered.

The poems of du Bouchet's last phase require an even more attentive reading, but the rewards are equal to the demands. More than any other poet, he persuades us to slow down, to give each syllable a chance. At first we may not realize what a passage like this, from "J'entrelettre ..." ("I Interletter . . .") might be evoking:

> one, all of sudden, and several.   whether swift or slow
> they strive to reach the blinding hearth.   the last isn't
> far, though blocked from my view and as hard to pick out as
> the fastest, which is ahead and has almost disappeared.

But a few lines later, the poet adverts to "running on the sun," and in retrospect we infer that these are clouds, racing toward that "blinding hearth." "Infer," because du Bouchet, especially in his final works, does not encourage us to fix on any single meaning. Many actions — and inactions — go on at once. In a landscape, through his words and his silent blanks, we are merely walking, seeing, and scribbling; but we are also approaching, assessing, and imagining. Then we flip back like acrobats to the primal level, where we walk, see, and scribble again. In his meditations on art we draw close to the work along with him, we look at every detail through his eyes, we hear him express what might be there. In his translations we accompany him again, we read, we absorb, we transmute. In every instance he helps us jettison our preconceptions, and reexperience the "mayhem of the torrents, purified at last."

All words are compacted metaphors, each with a past, present, and future: that is their enigma, and that is their strength. Every line of du Bouchet is so densely packed that he readily abandons the pretense of transparency. This brashness has given him the reputation of being "too difficult," even "unreadable," a charge he always confronted head on. In this regard another reminiscence comes to mind. Paul Auster and I first met du Bouchet in Paris at the beginning of the seventies, when we were both in our early twenties. At that time he was championing a translation by the equally young Pascal Quignard. He told us that some of his fellow editors at *L'Éphémère* considered it "too obscure" for the review—even though arcane ravings could only be expected from the poem's main narrator, Cassandra. It is indicative that in his 1970 lecture on Hölderlin in Stuttgart, du Bouchet compared the German poet's late work to "Cassandra's word, a word from which no lesson is to be drawn, a word, each time, and every time, spoken to say nothing . . . ." Fittingly, Auster used this pronouncement as an epigraph for his essay on du Bouchet of 1973 (see the Appendix at the end of our reader). It need hardly be emphasized that "nothing" in this context takes on a special meaning: a void that underlines itself as such, a word that radiates a negative pull, like a black hole that swallows the "somethings" of ordinary discourse.

While the original Greek of the *Cassandra* has been attributed to Lycophron of Chalcis, a Hellenistic poet, the author's true identity can only be described as moot. On his return to the United States Auster discovered that the work had been splendidly translated into English long ago by yet another young man about our age: Philip Lord Viscount Royston, who drowned in 1808 while voyaging in the Baltic Sea. Besides his version of Lycophron, the ill-fated traveler left behind letters addressed mainly to his father, the Earl of Hardwicke, as well as a lengthy poem on the subject of "Nothing"—not coincidentally, a central theme in du Bouchet's oeuvre, as we have noted. In the introduction to his Miltonic rendering of the *Cassandra*, Lord Royston squarely countered the usual disparagement of Lycophron's "obscurity." "Darkness is placed by Burke among the Sources of the Sublime . . . ," he asserted. "The sensations which are produced upon our minds by the absence of light are perhaps analogous to those which we feel when that mode of writing, metaphorically termed obscure, prevents the formation of distinct ideas, and sets no limits to our conceptions of *power.*"

In du Bouchet, this notion of power applies to the opaqueness of phenomena, physical or mental. If atoms, quarks, strings, and dark matter escape our notice, in the end they are no more unfathomable than morning light falling on a stone or the ricochets of a daydream. If he is truthful the poet can do no more, and no less, than mirror the conundrum of being itself. In one of his notebooks, du Bouchet jotted down the following lines:

> Readable
>
> poet . . .
>
>> I no more ask to be read
>> than reality.

And in the preface to his translation of excerpts from *Finnegans Wake*, he is even more adamant:

> *Finnegans Wake* immediately assumes its real dimension — expands — as soon as we set it aside. The unreadable is in fact the only infinity of which a work presenting itself as the written world can avail itself. This written world, which takes its measure from the living world in order to supplant it in the end, is stricken by the same muteness. Everything is transposed into words, and words will lapse back into silence. But Joyce dreams of seizing this ultimate silence in turn, and placing it at the heart of his narrative. This is the driving force of his persistence, of his brooding, of his inexplicable joy. And we feel it again and again in *Finnegans Wake* under the coinages of the unreadable, as under those of words plain to the point of truism, that well up from breakdown and collapse.

Du Bouchet's insistence on opacity, which impelled him to translate the late poems of Hölderlin's "madness" as well as the final works of Joyce, can best be explained by his own self-defining apothegm: "what holds us is what we cannot grasp."

But that is only half the story, as we have seen: otherwise, du Bouchet would have burned his notebooks as he had resolved, just as Wallace Stevens disposed of most of his drafts. Considering the alleged cryptic bent of his late period, we might whimsically compare du Bouchet's notebooks to Tzetzes' marginalia of Lycophron. But the French poet's annotations do not explicate, they are poems in their own right—though they may run parallel to other poems. From that standpoint, they resemble the commentary by San Juan de la Cruz on his own *Cántico spiritual:* poetry in prose that tangentially intersects with the ordered verses, allowing us to sense the hidden springs from which they flow. For example, in his lengthy gloss San Juan extols the Sierra Nevada landscape in sensuous detail, then abruptly avows: "These mountains are my Beloved for me." He is speaking of the divine, but its incarnation in nature is no less enigmatic than the ever-retreating threshold "outside" ourselves toward which all of du Bouchet's writing tends. His attachment to the late Hölderlin leads us in the same direction, toward the apprehension of a presence far beyond our ken, invoked in "Der Einzige" ("The Only One"—translated by du Bouchet as "L'unique") under the triune names of Heracles, Dionysus, and Christ. To echo Heidegger, all these intimations are "Holzwege," paths that lose themselves in forest depths.

Needless to say, there is no such thing as "mysticism" in du Bouchet's work, much less a personification of the sacred. Yet there is undeniably a profound strain of self-abnegation—without the overt links to Eastern teachings we find in Pierre-Albert Jourdan, another great diarist, whom John Taylor has translated with lucid care. Like Jourdan's harrowing account of his fatal cancer in "L'approche" ("The Approach"), du Bouchet's ardent passage toward the "outside" moves us all the more because he strips it of the masks that have so often consoled humankind. All he professes is that beyond our limits there is otherness, though that otherness rebounds into the mind itself, rapidly shuffling consciousness from absence to presence, from presence to absence, over and over again. In his remarks about the art of minting maxims, Jourdan stresses the import of the pause between each of them as a mindful act of restraint. By contrast, du Bouchet's ever-widening spaces denote the poetic process itself, its restless, serial attachment and detachment—to and from the external sphere, as well as to and from its own inner movements. To borrow a phrase from William Bronk, he invites us to experience each and every moment, within and without, as "the world, the worldless." As we advance through physical reality, we perambulate through thought: his poetry fuses the two indissolubly, yet also enacts the way each step erases the one that has gone before. Even so, these disappearing footfalls accumulate into a road, surging toward a goal which—as he acknowledges—will always elude us.

Like the poets of the late Renaissance, du Bouchet identifies mutability as the sole earthly truth—though he firmly rejects their ultimate appeal to a changeless beyond. Such unswerving fortitude in the face of life's essential futility cannot fail to impress us. But there is more here than courage: there is joy. As Paul Auster has noted in his essay, "What du Bouchet manages to maintain, almost uncannily, is a nostalgia for a possible future, even as he knows it will never come to pass. And from this dreadful knowledge, there is nevertheless a kind of joy, a joy . . . that is born of nothing." To this last phrase, drawn from du Bouchet's book of 1972, *Qui n'est pas tourné vers nous*—a title that says it all—I would add that the poet fully embraces his "dreadful knowledge" of the human dilemma as soon as he ascertains the silence "outside" all words, "outside" all existence. What du Bouchet concluded about Joyce applies to himself, once we grasp his entire corpus of writing as a unity: a "supreme fiction," but one that he shatters with ruthless honesty, creating an openwork as porous as life itself. In composing it he "dreams of seizing this ultimate silence in turn, and placing it at the heart of his narrative. This is the driving force of his persistence, of his brooding, of his inexplicable joy."

—Hoyt Rogers
Venice, 2014

Openwork

Part One: Early Poems and Notebooks

translated by Hoyt Rogers

AIR

À l'heure où la réalité coupe comme un morceau de vitre, on voit clairement les détails de la rue. Aussi reconnaissables qu'une chose jamais vue ni entendue. Quand la réalité se tait, comprenant alors qu'on est en dehors de la réalité, et qu'il faut y entrer. Il faut descendre et tout expliciter.

La page des vents éclaircie par le vent.

Mais la poésie semble à tel point en dehors de la vie, que si l'on se parlait couramment avec autant de clarté, personne ne se comprendrait.

On doit marcher. On ne peut pas s'attarder. À force de hausser la voix, on se lasse de parler.

Court-circuit de l'homme et du jour. Beaucoup trop court.

Que reste-t-il de tant de traits comme par hasard arrachés et soumis sans trêve à l'épreuve du réveil, de l'homme lui-même si abondamment raturé, piétiné, qui se détache si bien sur le trottoir? Le livre en brèche, les mots en hâte reprisés, les images qui roulent sous le front et le bruit de la voix. Vraiment, il faut relever la tête pour pouvoir respirer.

AIR

At the hour when reality cuts like a piece of glass, we clearly see the details of the street. Recognizable, like something never seen or heard. When reality falls silent, we grasp that we're outside it and need to get in. We have to go down and make everything plain.

The page of winds cleared up by the wind.

But poetry seems outside of life to such a point that if we routinely spoke with that much clarity, none of us would understand.

We have to walk. We cannot dawdle. By raising our voices, we weary of speech.

Short circuit of man and day. Far too short.

What's left of so many traits uprooted as though by chance and fed relentlessly to the waking ordeal? What's left of the man himself so thoroughly trampled and smudged out, whose outline on the sidewalk is so sharp? The dog-eared book, the words hastily darned, the images rolling under his brow and the sound of his voice. Truly, we must lift our heads in order to breathe.

JE NE VOIS PRESQUE RIEN

Le papier que je coupe
est moite
la montagne est presque cachée par son surplis blanc

Les mots se calment
et retrouvent leur assiette

L'air plus chaud que la peau

je sors enfin

ce n'est pas moi qui taille ces rues

tout existe si fort

I SEE ALMOST NOTHING

The paper I cut
is damp
the mountain almost hidden by its surplice of white

Words calm down
and find their ground

Air hotter than skin

at last I go out

I am not the one who carves these streets

everything exists, so strong

et loin
que je peux lâcher ma main

dehors

je ne vois presque rien.

and so far
I can let go of my hand

outside

I see almost nothing.

ALPHABET INCENDIE

Lettres noires grandes comme des oiseaux
et douces à l'œil, ce sont des histoires d'incendie
et la peur furtive d'avoir perdu son bien.

Nos remords sont nourris à force de vignettes.
Les plaisirs filtrés par la nuit deviennent amers :
c'est comme un sentiment qu'on éprouve à l'envers,
un reflet, tel est le calme enfer des arbres
dans la rivière claire, dont les branches se démêlent
en souriant : je récuse ce tendre alphabet.
Au feu, Au feu, et c'est toujours Au feu
et c'est toujours l'affolement de la chaîne
et la soif inutile et le feu dévorant.

ALPHABET FIRE

Black letters big as birds
and sweet to the eye: stories of fire,
and the sneaking fear we've lost what we love.

Our remorse feeds on scenes that we rehearse.
Pleasures filtered by night turn to brine,
like a feeling we experience upside-down:
a mirror-image, such is the placid hell of trees
in the gleaming brook. Their branches smile,
dangle free: but I refuse this tender alphabet.
Burn, Burn, and always Burn
and forever the frenzy of chains
and pointless thirst and ravenous fire.

FEUILLES DU JOUR

Le premier coup résonne interminablement sur la boîte
     métallique
on entend tout ce qui respire
l'or glacé du réverbère tremble dans le bain
poitrine aveuglée
toi voix de l'air happé par l'air
toi sourde
tournant
et roulant encore une fois dans la chambre.

LEAVES OF DAY

The first blow echoes forever on the metal box
we hear everything that breathes
the lamppost's icy gold quivers in the bath
blinded chest
you—a voice of air swallowed by air
you—deaf
turning
and rolling in the room once more.

CHAMBRE

J'ai vu une porte flamber en pleine nuit comme un soleil.

Je ne peux pas sortir de la chambre avant qu'elle-même, la terre, ne soit lame de la terre.

Le jour gagne les draps, l'étoffe blanche allumée. Mur aveugle, sourd. Pierraille au-dessus de ce feu muet, la grande tasse d'eau de l'aube. Le brasier dévore le ciel en silence, comme un planeur. Il faut dire qu'il n'y a pas de cris, pas de voix. Tout se tait dehors, dans la tête, par terre et les pierres.

Lumière aigre de la première lampe.

Le soc rouge. Feu sans chaleur, lumière glacée, chaleur sans voix.

Nous marchons en pleine laine, dans une vague sourde.

Avant que la chaleur ne grésille, quand elle est sans mouches, sans chaleur.

ROOM

In the thick of night I saw a door blazing like a sun.

I cannot leave the room till the earth itself becomes the blade of earth.

Daylight spreads to the sheets, kindling white cloth. Wall— blind, deaf. Gravel above this speechless fire, the great water-cup of dawn. The brazier eats the sky in silence, like a burnisher. We hear no voices, no shouts. Nothing makes a sound outside—within our head, or on the ground and the stones.

The curdling light of the first lamp.

The red plowshare. Heatless fire, frozen light, voiceless heat.

We walk through heavy wool, in a muffled wave.

Before the heat sizzles—no flies, no heat.

VOCABLE

Tout devient mots
terre
cailloux

dans ma bouche et sous mes pas

homme repris
tendu
en pierres
en pièces
d'or

monnaie des mots et des pas

ce que je te dis te fait rire

or
sans nom qui me monnaie
vivant.

TERM

Everything becomes words
earth
pebbles

in my mouth and under my feet

man given back
redeemed
in stones
in coins
of gold

currency of words and steps

what I say makes you laugh

nameless
gold that barters me
alive.

« LES ÉPINES DÉCHIRANTES ... »

[d'un carnet de 1951]

Les épines déchirantes, les glaçons transparents de la connaissance dans la lumière fade du jour et du rêve.

Écrire lorsqu'on ne trouve devant soi que cette paroi muette qui ne répond pas. Écrire parce qu'on n'a plus rien à dire; c'est à ce moment, de tous le plus mauvais, qu'il faut le dire.

Je me trouve encore devant moi : il faut passer.

C'est l'immensité qui m'arrête. Indicible sensation d'étouffement devant la réalité qui me fait repartir. Je recommence, je crie derrière cette muraille de mots qui s'écarte lentement et va se refermer derrière moi ; on voulait sortir : on est simplement passé dans une autre pièce.

Écrire ce texte devrait chaque fois être aussi facile que respirer. Chaque fois, il faut que je me lance violemment en avant, comme dans un bain glacé. Mon état usuel est donc l'asphyxie.

Voici les quelques phrases qui survivent au poème que j'ai oublié et qui a disparu avec le soleil.

Tout a été dit, mais il faut sans cesse le répéter.

"THE PIERCING THORNS . . ."

[from a notebook of 1951]

The piercing thorns, the clear ice-floes of awareness in the vapid light of day and dreams.

Writing when all we find before us is this mute wall that does not answer. Writing because there is nothing left to say; that's the moment, the worst moment of all, when we have to say it.

I still find myself in front of myself: I must move on.

It's the immensity that stops me. The untellable sense of choking on reality that makes me set out again. I start over, I shout behind this wall of words that slowly parts, and will close behind me once more. We wanted to go outside: all we did was enter another room.

Writing this text each time should come as naturally as breathing. Each time, I have to thrash wildly ahead, as if in freezing water. Which means my usual state is suffocation.

Here are the few surviving phrases from the poem I have forgotten, and that vanished with the sun.

Everything has been said, but we have to repeat it again and again.

Horreur de voir ces choses se composer en mots.

Deux poésies : celle qui s'élabore pendant que l'homme reste muet, les mots faits de beaucoup de silence ; et celle qui emboîte la parole au héros.

La terre somnambule. L'air imprimé que la nuit remue.

*

Payer de mots. Le silence ne donne que le silence.

Chaque poème est une écorce arrachée qui met les sens à vif. Le poème a rompu cette taie, ce mur, qui atrophie les sens. On peut alors saisir un instant la terre, la réalité. Puis la plaie vive se cicatrise. Tout redevient sourd, aveugle, muet.

Saisir l'homme, aussi réel que la nature. La conscience qui flambe sans mots.

Au lieu de commencer par former des mots, des phrases, j'imagine d'abord des rapports muets avec le monde.

L'assemblage préalable des mots facilite la tâche, mais rend le poème plus lâche.

The horror of seeing these things arrange themselves into words.

Two forms of poetry: the one that takes shape while the poet says nothing, words made of much silence; and the one that molds its words around the hero.

The sleepwalking earth. The printed air stirred by night.

＊

Paying with words. Silence gives only silence.

Every poem is a ripped-off piece of bark that flays the senses. The poem has broken this casing, this wall, which atrophies the senses. For an instant we can grasp the earth, grasp reality. Then the open wound heals over. Everything goes deaf again, goes mute and blind.

To take hold of man, as real as nature. A mind blazing without words.

Instead of creating words and sentences, I begin by imagining my silent connection with the world.

Assembling words beforehand makes the task easier, but the poem becomes more cowardly.

La lamentation, l'invective et l'interrogation ont été remplacées par la définition. Rien d'étonnant à ce que les poèmes tendent à être plus concis.

Si l'on pouvait forcer la nature à parler : toutes les hyperboles viennent de là. Forcer la nature comme on force un coffre — la nature muette.

Battement éternel entre les textes largement ouverts, évocateurs d'objets réfractaires à la parole, et ces dix lignes fermées comme le poing.

Il fallait creuser dans les mots, dans le jour, un espace analogue à celui de cette chambre, par exemple.

L'homme est la partie consciente de la réalité, il est la tête de la réalité.

Lamentation, invective, and interrogation have been supplanted by the impulse to define. Hardly surprising that poems tend to be more concise.

If we could force nature to speak: all hyperboles spring from that. Pry nature open as we pry open a chest—speechless nature.

Eternal back-and-forth between wide-open texts, redolent with objects that balk at words, and these ten lines as tight as a fist.

We need to hollow out in words, in broad daylight, a space analogous to this room, for example.

Man is the conscious part of reality; man is reality's head.

« POÈTE LISIBLE … »

[d'un carnet daté du 5 mai 1953]

>   Poète
> lisible
>   moi qui ne demande pas plus à être lu
>   que la réalité

>   crois-tu que nous puissions vivre ainsi

. . .

En fait, je veux me maintenir dans un état de pauvreté et non
de connaissance par rapport au monde.

. . .

mon rêve
la tête pleine de terre
dans le brouillage formidable du vent
heureux jusqu'à la cime

. . .

Je sais fort bien différencier la réalité du goût qu'elle me
     donne

Poésie —
         ce miracle —

le secret en superficie : ce qu'il y a de plus secret, d'unique,
croirait-on, au grand jour, et mis en commerce grâce à ce lan-
gage banal — comme si même elle ne pouvait prendre con-
science de son secret que par cette mesure publique — l'homme

"READABLE POET . . ."

[from a notebook dated May 5, 1953]

    Readable

poet . . .

        I no more ask to be read

        than reality

        do you think we can live like that

. . .

In fact, I want to keep myself in a state of poverty and not
of knowledge in relation to the world.

. . .

my dream

my head full of earth

in the awesome scrambling of the wind

happy all the way to the crown

. . .

I know quite well how to distinguish reality from the taste it
    gives me

Poetry—

        this miracle—

the secret on the surface: what is most secret, unique, or so
you'd assume, in broad daylight, and circulated through this
ordinary language—as though it could only become aware of
its secret through this public measure—man

c'est donner un nouveau goût au jour pour les autres hommes
cette réalité qu'il tire de lui-même, de lui qui n'est que la
    lampe
des autres hommes, qu'un homme accru, et pour les autres
hommes
représentant l'homme : les mots si simples se doublent, se
répercutent — jour — pain — avec une force accrue —
la faim comblée par ce désintéressement —

il le tire de lui-même mais à ce moment, il représente les
    autres hommes

en réalité, rien ne peut être trop clair

la poésie peut être trop claire — on ne voit rien

il faut que l'œil s'habitue

moi, émissaire de la réalité
qu'elle envoie comme émissaire

« la terre est sous les mots comme un champ sous les
    mouches » :
mots visualisés

mon plus grand désir est de me banaliser, à partir de cette
impuissance — près avoir tenu compte de mon impuissance

it means giving others a new taste of what daylight is
this reality that he draws from himself, he who is only the lamp
of others, a man increased, and for
all others
he represents man: the simple words are doubled,
echoed—day—bread—with strength increased—
hunger fulfilled by this abnegation—

he draws it from himself but at that moment, he represents all
the others

in reality, nothing can be too clear

poetry can be too clear—you see nothing

the eye must get used to it

I, the envoy of reality
sent by reality

"the earth is under words like a field under flies":
words visualized

my greatest desire is to make myself ordinary, out of being
powerless—after reckoning with my lack of power

— de remonter cet immense courant
que mon ancienne impuissance colore et donne un reflet
nouveau à tout ce que je pourrais dire de banal — mais que
     ce
qui est banal, je le dise.
Car mes poèmes, c'est bien ce à quoi je suis devenu aveugle,
encore plus qu'au monde réel.

            des yeux : qui ont perdu leur vertu après avoir
servi — pour moi, du moins —

ils ne peuvent voir que par d'autres

la poésie : perdre sa personnalité

—to swim back up this immense current
so my old helplessness will color, will give a new
gleam to every ordinary thing I could say—and whatever
    might be
ordinary, I will say it.
Because it is precisely to my poems that I have gone blind,
even more than to the real world.

                    eyes: that lost their power after having
served—for me, at least—

they cannot see except through others

poetry: losing your personality

« ET TA MAIN PASSE SUR LES YEUX OUVERTS … »

[d'un carnet daté du 19 juillet 1953]

et ta main passe sur les yeux ouverts
comme une tasse d'eau

l'air décimé
quelques branches décimées — nous prenons goût à la vie

des meules
des flaques
dont notre ciel s'éclaire

et je me retourne tout à coup
pour surprendre le ciel

          . . .

quelques pas
      et je te perds
dans la terre redoutable
qui s'est levée

la terre fauve

          . . .

nous étions terre retournée
nous nous retrouvions seuls
contre l'air

      et je m'étonne de me retrouver ce qu'un enfant avait

"AND YOUR HAND PASSES OVER OPEN EYES . . ."

[from a notebook dated July 19, 1953]

and your hand passes over open eyes
like a cup of water

the decimated air
a few decimated boughs—we start enjoying life

haystacks
puddles
lighting up our sky

and suddenly I wheel around
to surprise the sky

. . .

a few steps
    and I lose you
in the daunting earth
that has risen up

the wild earth

. . .

we were the tilled ground
we found ourselves alone
against the air

and I am amazed to find I have become what a child had

voulu devenir

. . .

je voulais que mon poème s'écrive sans moi

. . .

Un instant, nous avons été aussi réels qu'un mur. Nous
pouvions mourir.

. . .

mon enfance
            est en haut
        sous la poussière

. . .

je m'enfonce dans la route
— dans l'enfer

. . .

nous nous décidions
nous nous dessinions

. . .

dans cette immensité
        où notre feu tire sur la laisse

nous n'avons pas un instant

. . .

l'air a repris son vrai visage

un peu plus haut
        là où les arbres sont brûlés

wanted to become

. . .

I wanted my poem to write itself without me

. . .

For an instant, we have been as real as a wall. We were able
    to die.

. . .

my childhood
                is up there
        under the dust

. . .

I plunge into the road
—into hell

. . .

we were making up our minds
we were taking shape

. . .

in this immensity
        where our fire pulls on the leash

we don't have an instant

. . .

the air has taken on its true face again

a little higher
        where the trees are burned

où la cendre des arbres se dissipe

où les branches se sont brusquement arrêtées

un enfant crie autant que le vent

c'est le même brassage

une flamme du même feu
auquel nous nous plions
je suis là
je brûle

et je reviens pour en parler

la terre piquée d'arbres
et le ciel vide

le ciel rempli de phrases éteintes

et partout il se promène
avec ce feu aigre
comme des piquants

. . .

vraiment
nous étions dans tout ce qu'il y a avait de plus haut

et le vent secouait la vitre

where the ash of the trees subsides

where the branches have abruptly stopped

a child shouts as much as the wind

it's the same mingling

a flame of the same fire
to which we bow
I am there
I burn

  and I come back to tell the tale

the earth spiked by trees
  and the empty sky

the sky filled with burnt-out phrases

and it walks around everywhere
  with this fire, sharp
as spikes

  . . .

truly
  we were in all that was most high

and the wind shook the windowpane

j'étais livré au jour
      sans choix
      sans goût
      sans soif

           . . .

les aboiements dans l'air
tendu comme un tambour

           . . .

je retrouve un instant dehors
la morale d'avant les moissons — la raison du vent

     dans le champ délivré de sa récolte

       et un instant vacant

I was surrendered to the light
       without choice
       without craving
       without thirst

          . . .

a barking in the air
tight as a drum

          . . .

the moment I'm outside I recover
the morale from before the harvests—the reason for the wind

    in the field delivered of its harvest

    and now suddenly vacant

« LA COHÉRENCE PROFONDE ... »

[de la fin du même carnet]

La cohérence profonde de certaines images superficielles, disparates, d'où elles tirent leur pouvoir d'évidence — tout en demeurant sourdes et mates — n'étant que le reflet de la fidélité à une évidence extérieure — dont souvent il ne reste plus trace — comme un poème aussitôt qu'il cesse d'être lié à l'effort du poète

cette cohérence qui nous fait admettre un poème aveuglément — aussi aveuglément que la réalité — et leur confère la même nature rudimentaire

on peut bien dire que par rapport à cette réalité, nous n'avons pas avancé d'un pas, et Rimbaud s'y est tout autant conformé.

C'est surtout par rapport à l'imagination que l'on peut dire que l'on avance — haute ou faible imagination — trouvant également son répondant dans la réalité — exaltante ou écœurante

ainsi les plus beaux poèmes ont abouti à quelques textes blancs comme une page de papier blanche — sont disponibles : c'est-à-dire qu'ils n'ont pas cessé d'agir. Comme tout ce qui s'est mis à agir.

J'écris toujours pour me rendre digne du poème qui n'est pas encore écrit.
Sans espoir.

"THE PROFOUND COHERENCE . . ."

[from the end of the same notebook]

The profound coherence of certain superficial, ill-assorted images, from which they clearly draw their power—while they remain muted and dull—merely reflects fidelity to outward evidence—of which often no trace is left—like a poem as soon as it stops being bound to the poet's striving

this coherence that makes us blindly accept a poem—as blindly as reality—and confers on both the same rudimentary nature

it could be said that in regard to this reality we have made no headway at all, and Rimbaud was no different from the others.

It's above all in regard to the imagination that we can say we're making headway—imagination, whether lofty or weak—also finding its echo in the real—whether exalting or repugnant

and so the most beautiful poems have led to some blank texts like a sheet of blank paper—are available: that is, they have not ceased to act. Like everything that has begun to act.

I always write to make myself worthy of the poem that is not yet written.
Without hope.

« À MES PIEDS ... »

[d'un carnet daté du 15 août 1953]

à mes pieds, je suis sur une nappe encore colorée et vivante
malgré la nuit—comme un souffle plat—
j'écarte les fruits

les mots mûrs

comme ma fille me dit
c'est rouge
après s'être coupé le doigt

"AT MY FEET . . ."

[from a notebook dated August 15, 1953]

at my feet, I'm on a cloth still colorful and vivid
in spite of the night—like a flattened breath—
I set aside the fruits

     ripe words

as my daughter said
it's red
after cutting her finger

à un morceau de pierre

la force radicale
qui nous pétrit
une grande force
fraîche
sans traits
et ne vivant que par nos traits

qu'elle saisit

sans ce tourment sourd et aveugle

comme un enfant
        qui joue
            avec des pierres
dès que sa mère l'a quitté

je me suis trouvé seul
devant un mur

            . . .
        je l'ai rencontrée dehors
elle m'a suivi.
            jusqu'à la pièce où nous nous sommes empoignés

[et je l'ai] appelée mon amour

on a chunk of stone

the radical force
that kneads us
a great force
fresh
featureless
and living only by our features

     which it seizes

without this deaf and blind torment

like a child
    who plays
     with stones
as soon as her mother has left her

I found myself alone
before a wall

     . . .

    I met up with my wife outside
she followed me.

     to the room where we had a fight

[and I] called her my love

nous avons connu cette merveille
être séparés

une pierre
        d'une admirable couleur bleue

je te remercie
        mon tourment

de la permission de vivre

j'avais dormi toute la nuit dans ce feu

sans dormir
        j'étais près de mourir

we have known this marvel
being separate

a stone
        of an exquisite shade of blue

I thank you
        my torment

for the permission to live

I had slept all night in this fire

without sleeping
        I came close to dying

mais ma mort ne m'appartenait pas

comme la clarté
                    surgissant
            de la nuit blanche
n'appartient pas à la nuit,
mon amour.

but death did not belong to me

as the brightness
                 rising
        from the white night
does not belong to the night,
my love.

« COMME UN HOMME ... »

[d'un carnet daté du 23 août 1953]

comme un homme
dans un jour sans soleil
qui resplendit
vivant
presque
en dehors de l'air

. . .

ce que j'écris me gêne autant que mon corps

c'est une lampe blanche

toujours allumée

même quand la lumière est inutile
et qu'il fait jour

et je me perds inutilement dans le jour

mais pour peu que j'insiste
je trouve   ma destruction

et je vois   par ce cadre

je ne suis pas mort

"LIKE A MAN . . ."

[from a notebook dated August 23, 1953]

like a man
in a day without sun
that glows
alive
almost
outside the air

. . .

what I write bothers me as much as my body

it is a white lamp

always lit

even when its light is useless
and day has come

and uselessly I lose myself in the day

but should I insist
I would find   my destruction

and I see   by this arrangement

I am not dead

je marche   jusqu'à la fin du jour

sans traîner derrière

comme il faut quitter le sol
            pour qu'il se détache

                        . . .

chaque fois qu'on rit, on touche le fond de la réalité

                        . . .

Parfois, j'ai la joie de découvrir que je suis très en arrière de ce
que j'ai déjà fait.

Je me hâte de repartir en avant.

                        . . .

Romantique:
Je ne peux pas m'empêcher d'incarner ce que je sais
            c'est mon mal.

Je retrouve mes épaules
                    comme une pierre

devant mon mal

c'est que ma vérité
ma sincérité
est encore en dehors de moi

I walk   till the end of day

without falling behind

as you have to leave the ground
        for the ground to let go

                    . . .

every time we laugh, we get to the bottom of reality

                    . . .

Sometimes, I have the joy of discovering that I am far behind
what I have already done.

I hasten to get ahead again.

                    . . .

Romantic:
I cannot help but incarnate what I know
        is my illness.

I find my shoulders
            like a stone

before my illness

it's that my truth
my sincerity
is still outside myself

je ne l'incarne pas
elle se trouve plutôt dans mes amis

et toi
        ma femme perdue

je te vois encore
        comme une lame éclatée
dans l'encadrement de la porte

le temps de penser à toi
et de t'avoir vue disparaître
tu étais devenue fine et coupante
  comme une lame

           . . .

je voudrais vivre
        ayant vu
et que voir
      suffise

devenir pays

tirer ma vertu d'une route ou d'un fleuve

être champ
et soc de ce champ

et que ce champ travaille pour moi

I do not incarnate it
it is found instead in my friends

and you
                my lost wife

I still see you
            like a shattered blade
in the frame of the door

the time of thinking of you
and having seen you disappear
you had become as thin and cutting
  as a blade

                        . . .

I would like to live
                having seen
and seeing
                should be enough

to become a country

drawing my worth from a river or a road

to be a field
and the plowshare of that field

so that field will work for me

. . .

j'intercale du papier blanc
pour me reposer

. . .

La poésie, c'est le prix d'une réalité animée — la douleur d'une
nature animée. Et sans doute, à défaut du reste, cette douleur
est-elle vraie

la douleur de ce qui se déchire pour s'animer

je n'ai que cela à faire, et je ne fais que cela

poésie — ce qu'on aime — comme le public, surtout sensible
à la cadence — généralement écrite beaucoup plus tard — du
concerto, lui réel, qui donne le terrain, le sol irréfutable d'où
cette cadence se détache — ainsi de l'influence exercée par une
poésie qui se dissipe justement dans cette influence

. . .

I insert a blank sheet of paper
in order to find some rest

. . .

Poetry is the price of an enlivened reality—the pain of an enliv-
ened nature. And undoubtedly, all else failing, this pain is genu-
ine

the pain of what tears itself apart in order to come alive

that is all I have to do, and that is all I do

poetry—what people love—like the audience, responsive
above all to the cadenza—generally written much later—of
the concerto, itself real, which gives the ground, the irrefut-
able grounding from which that cadenza removes itself—such
is the influence wielded by a poetry that in this very influence
fades away

« CE BALBUTIEMENT BLANC ... »

[d'un carnet daté de 4 fevrier 1954]

ce balbutiement blanc

      la terrible assurance de la réalité

et cette bulle

      la figure du jour
         ravagé

           . . .

présente
    et absente

c'est un cri d'amour

        devant toi
je te parle
comme si tu n'étais pas là.

        et comme si
          m'enfonçant dans la vérité
je me retrouvais seul.

        et sans toi

"THIS BLANK STUTTERING . . ."

[from a notebook dated February 4, 1954]
this blank stuttering

     the dreadful confidence of reality

and this bubble

     the face of ravaged
        day

           . . .

present
   and absent

it is a cry of love

        in front of you
I speak to you
as if you weren't there.

       and as if
         plunging into the truth
I found myself alone.

          and without you

la mort
la vérité
                      et de nouveau je suis vivant
j'ai eu le sentiment de toute une éternité

cette fraîcheur
cette mort

              que j'exhale
avec promptitude
                      je suis vivant
                              . . .
Il faut que mon
poème reste ouvert
              et immobile

ouvert et immobile
                      comme une pierre
ouvert
et tenant tête au jour
                              . . .
J'attendais
              d'avoir perdu tout sentiment

              comme un être brut

              de recueillir

death
truth
         and once again I am alive
I had the feeling of a whole eternity

this coolness
this death

   which I promptly
exhale
         I am alive

       . . .

My poem must
remain open
     and unmoving

open and unmoving
       like a stone
open
and facing up to the light

       . . .

I expected
   to have lost all feeling

   like a brute

   to gather

ce feu qui vient à pied
sans chaleur

que je reconnais à sa lumière

et à sa main,
pareille à la main de l'air que nous respirons

this fire that comes on foot
without warmth

which I recognize by its light

and by its hand,
not unlike the hand of the air we breathe

« J'AI VU LE TRAIN AGRANDI ... »

[d'un carnet daté du 12 mars 1955]

J'ai vu le train agrandi par les terres

    train Venise — Grèce

un morceau d'astre agrandi, gonflé
à moitié enfoncé dans l'étendue noire

et l'accélération incompréhensible sous les nuages — sur le
fer lisse

comme tout s'imbrique
sans que pourtant nous soyons sortis de la terre — de cette
bulle d'air réservée

Mais pour qui voit l'air un peu en dehors de la route, la route
se perd.

sous le dôme de l'air

Puis ici, arrêtés en pleine nuit, en pleine campagne

en pays de laine —

"I SAW THE TRAIN ENLARGED . . ."

[from a notebook dated March 12, 1955]
I saw the train enlarged by the land

     train Venice—Greece

an enlarged splinter of star, swollen
half-submerged in the black expanse

and the gathering speed, uncanny under the clouds—on the
slick iron

how everything is interwoven
though we haven't yet emerged from the earth—from this
reserved bubble of air

But whoever sees the air a bit beyond the path, for him the
path is lost.

under the dome of air

Then here, stopped in the dead of night, in the heart

of wool country—

enfoncée dans les champs
— aux approches des montagnes, le feu s'éloigne, s'atténue

. . .

nous sommes affranchis
et attachés à la lumière
puis l'air froid nous sépare de la pierre —
le jour s'arrachant à nous, venant de la montagne déchirée —

nous avions encore reconnu le point où nous devions nous
séparer

devant l'eau noire, ruisselante

. . .

de temps en temps, une incursion hors de l'homme, dans l'air
sans front.

Hors des murs —

puis encore la main de buée du jour qui s'abaisse avant le soir
— environnés de cette blanche respiration
d'un souffle proche et froid qui nous étend.

d'un souffle proche du bâtiment

ici, mon dieu, il n'y a que cette vague noire qui passe
    lentement.

embedded in the fields
—at the edge of the mountains, the fire retreats, dies down

. . .

we are freed from
and attached to the light
then the cold air detaches us from stone—
the day tearing away from us, issuing from the shattered
    mountain—

we had still recognized the point where we had to
separate

before the streaming black water

. . .

from time to time, a foray outside the human, in the headless
air.

Outside the walls—

then again the light's steam, a hand that lowers before
    evening
—we are encircled by that white breathing,
by a breath, close and cold, that widens us.

by a breath close to the building

here, my god, there's nothing but this black wave that slowly
    passes.

Le cœur, ce tourbillon.

Le cœur — creusé.

Le bois sur le billot. Les traits du ravin que quitte le torrent,
l'air qui anime. Puis nous rentrons dans le feu de plusieurs
visages perdus —

au coin de la lanière éteinte de la terre.

J'ai dévisagé la route.

                              . . .

j'ai vu la terre deux fois se contracter

    son regard frôler le regard de l'eau

        me parvient ici, ce qui n'est pas séparé de ce qui est
        perdu

la pierre froide et la pierre chaude se répondent

la pierre interrompue
                    par une pierre neuve

                              . . .

Ton visage à côté de moi,
terre.

The heart, this whirlwind.
The heart—hollowed out.
Wood on the chopping block. The gully's features, left behind
by the torrent, the quickening air. Then we enter the fire of
    several
lost faces again—
at the edge of the dull belt of earth.

I stared the road down.

                    . . .

twice I have seen the earth shrink

    seen its gaze brush the water's gaze

    what reaches me here has not parted with what is lost

stones, cold and hot, answer each to each

the rock interrupted
                by new rock

                    . . .

Your face next to me,
earth.

Après que le froid nous a accueillis.

Seul, la nuit — ou depuis toutes les nuits — ton visage dans
mon ciel, dans ma tête.

ton visage aux yeux fermés

il y a, dans la sécheresse, de l'eau bleue
qui te fixe.

After the cold has welcomed us.

Alone, at night—or for all the nights—your face in
my sky, in my head.

your face with eyes closed

there is, in the dryness, blue water
staring at you.

« ICI LE JOUR S'ACCORDE ... »

[d'un carnet daté du 5 août 1955]

ici le jour s'accorde à mon pas.

je glisse à la fois sur la neige du papier et sur cette terre sèche.

sans avoir encore connu le répit

je débouche toujours au même sommet —
je mets plusieurs semaines à me retrouver à ce sommet.

. . .

l'air qui nous interrompit
        et nous agrandit

une paroi qui naît au contact de l'horizon
et se disperse

comme les quatre murs du jour où je suis enfermé
qui parfois se rejoignent et font une seule paroi devant
    laquelle
je me retrouve — dehors.

. . .

Le soir venu, l'embrasure est plus blanche. L'horizon est proche
du seuil de la pièce où je suis perdu.

. . .

Je ne porte sur le corps que cette lettre à laquelle je tiens et
qui n'a plus de nom — dont il ne reste que le ciel qui sépare
les lignes.

"HERE THE LIGHT FALLS IN STEP . . ."

[from a notebook dated August 5, 1955]
here the light falls in step with me.

.

I slide on the snow of the paper, I slide on this dry earth.

without any respite so far

I always end up at the same summit—
I spend several weeks to get there again.

. . .

the air cuts us short
            and expands us

a barrier born when it strikes the horizon
and scatters

like the four walls of day that enclose me
that join sometimes into a single wall in front of which
I find myself—outside.

. . .

As evening falls, the doorway whitens. The horizon is close to
the threshold of the room where I am lost.

. . .

All I carry on my body is this letter I cherish, which no longer
has a name—of which nothing is left but the sky between the
lines.

. . .

Si la terre continue de souffler, nous serons nous-mêmes usés.

J'ai connu le jour que rien ne distingue du précédent
et qui pourtant se déchaîne, se dresse comme un mur
      écrasant,
et se retourne contre nous. Sans que rien au-dehors
      transparaisse.

Je me répéterai comme la terre qu'on foule.

dans l'éclat d'un jour nouveau

je suis couché dans une longue traînée de cendre — mes doigts
deviennent gris comme des brindilles brûlées, et noirs aux join-
tures

le vent la fait au début un peu voler autour de moi — puis nous
[nous] assagissons ensemble.

. . .

je me résous comme un arbre dans le jour

ce sont mes membres qui se défont

je sais que je marche vers un soir que je porte au creux de la
poitrine

. . .

. . .

If the earth keeps breathing hard, we will wear ourselves out.

I have known a day just like the one before it
but that rages, towers like a crushing wall,
turning against us. With nothing showing on the surface.

I will repeat myself like the earth we walk on.

in the burst of a new day

I am lying in a long trail of ash—my fingers
turn gray like burnt twigs, and black
at the joints—

first the wind swirls the ash around me a bit—then
we quiet down together.

. . .

I take a stand like a tree in the light

it's my limbs that go slack

I know I am walking toward an evening that I carry in the hollow of my chest

. . .

Je reviens du fin fond des terres — jusqu'à ces confins — à
l'heure où le jour brûle encore sur les bords —
ou y fait courir un cordon de feu

I return from the ends of the earth—to this borderland—
at the hour when the edges of day still burn—
or ring it with a cordon of fire

« QUAND NOUS NE SOMMES QUE PRISONNIERS … »

[d'un carnet daté du 12 novembre 1955]

quand nous ne sommes que prisonniers de cette vie

et des parois de cette vie

rien

sortir — ce n'est pas sortir —

si
chaque jour
nous avons vécu d'une vie

nous avons vécu mille vies brèves — coupées net le soir —
    par
la faux, sur le sol froid du soir.

le silence aussi donne le sol
              . . .
Tu connais la terre suffisante — et celle qui soudain se
    démasque
et ne te suffit plus —

              . . .

"WHEN WE'RE ONLY PRISONERS . . ."

[from a notebook dated November 12, 1955]

when we're only prisoners of this life

and the walls of this life

nothing

going out—is not going out—

if
each day
we have lived a life

we have lived a thousand brief lives—cut down at evening—
    by
the scythe, on the cold ground of evening.

silence also gives ground

. . .

You know the sufficiency of earth—and the earth that
    suddenly unmasks itself
as not sufficient—

. . .

Mais je me souviens de ma vie comme de la terre lorsque je ne sors pas.

. . .

Je n'ai pas crié, je n'ai pas pleuré en retrouvant ma tête rase — et ce qui, de moi, reste toujours à brûler

. . .

J'ai profité de cet état de grande faiblesse — j'ai marché — de cette faiblesse heureuse

la force humaine et la faiblesse terrestre cessent d'être distinctes

la lumière est cet être de grande faiblesse qui sait sourdre de la terre

. . .

ma ponctuation est la bêche avec laquelle j'avance dans le champ — bêche qui ouvre le champ —
            et le fracas surgi par toutes les portes humaines.

quand cette angoisse me quitte, je m'immobilise —
quand elle me rejoint, je marche —
coupé en deux, je me dédouble dans la lumière

je demeure à l'horizon

. . .

ce qui se détache de la terre éclaire la terre

mais nous sommes vraiment loin des lieux interpellés —

But I remember my life as I remember the earth when I don't
go out.

. . .

I didn't shout, I didn't cry when I found my head was
    shaved—
and found what within me still remains to be burned

. . .

I've taken advantage of this great weakness—I've walked—of
this happy weakness

human strength and earthly weakness are no longer different

light is a being of great weakness, which knows how to well up
from the earth

. . .

my punctuation is the spade I take with me into the field—
the spade that opens up the field—
        and the din that pours out through all human doors.

when this anguish leaves me, I stand still—
when it comes back, I walk—
cut in two, I split up in the light

I remain on the horizon

. . .

what detaches itself from the earth illumines the earth

but we are truly far from the clamor—

malgré cette perpétuelle commotion —

    notre main friable, glacée — nos doigts cassants le
      disent

et la marche reprend —
et les arbres, les arbustes repartent avec moi —
la moire de la terre tourne et s'immobilise autour de moi
avec un grand battement

     . . .

à portée de main, la puissance du ciel sur un tas de pierres —
sur le réflecteur d'un amas de pierres froides

la terre, comme une aile immense dans le vent
planant au-dessus de la terre

     . . .

les corbeaux, les glaciers qui grincent

     . . .

comme si je cherchais la parole extérieure

des fruits qui tiennent encore à l'arbre noir
dans le sens opposé au couchant

alors en nous tournant dans le vent froid
c'est toute l'assiette du visage qui nous est révélée

comme une surface froide et plate

despite this unending commotion—

       our crushable, frozen hand—our brittle fingers say so

and the walk resumes—
and the trees, the bushes set out with me again—
the mottled cloth of earth wheels around me and stands still
with a vast, single thrum

      . . .

at hand, the power of the sky on a pile of stones—
on a mirroring heap of cold stones

the earth, like an enormous wing in the wind
hovering above the earth

      . . .

crows, the glaciers that creak

      . . .

as if I were searching for words that are not within me

fruits that still cling to the black tree
on the opposite side of sunset

then as we turn in the cold wind
we find the platter of our face wholly revealed

as a surface cold and flat

au-dessus de la route

. . .

des tronçons
        et chaque intervalle
est une montagne

un tronçon de distance — comme du bois à brûler
    oui égarés
    dispersés

mais nous avons trouvé
        dans notre déchirement
un tel champ

la brume qui monte
le matin
enveloppe notre front

mille apparitions
        mille arpents

mille lieux froids et morts
qui scintillent

        le jour
sur terre

. . .

La lumière n'apparaît plus avant le milieu du jour

above the road

. . .

chunks
        and each interval
is a mountain

a chunk of distance — like firewood
   yes they are mislaid
   scattered

but we have found them
            in our heartbreak
such a field

the mist as it rises
in the morning
shrouds our forehead

a thousand apparitions
        a thousand acres

a thousand places cold and dead
that glitter

        daylight
on earth

. . .

The light no longer appears before the middle of day

. . .

le jour est comme une lame — sur le champ

cette faux, quand il n'y a rien à couper — et qu'elle reste, hors
de saison, sur la terre.

pour rouler

dans la chambre aride, dans la chambre précaire de dehors

je ne peux sortir sans trouver — encore une fois — cette
     grande
porte ouverte devant moi — cette grande porte sans battants

. . .

mais notre amour qui a perdu sa forme
et son nom dans le vent —
          comme un champ

notre amour — le vent

cet amour plat et transparent comme le vent.

je me suis retrouvé autre dans le jour différent

. . .

amour — comme la terre — non moins démesuré

. . .

la joie — c'était de voir mon front, la tête qui se perdait sous
le ciel, comme un talus, l'herbe et le souffle rêche mêlés

. . .

the day is like a blade—on the field

this scythe, when there is nothing to cut—and it stays, out of
season, on the earth.

    to roll

in the parched room, in the precarious room of outdoors

I can't go out without finding—once again—this vast
door open before me—this vast doorway without doors

. . .

but our love which has lost its shape
and its name in the wind—
    like a field

    our love—the wind

this love flat and transparent like the wind.

I seemed altered in the different day

. . .

love—like the earth—no less enormous

. . .

joy—it was seeing my brow, the head that was vanishing
under the sky, like a slope of grass mingled with rasping
   breath

de voir ce talus

de le voir de loin

encore en vie

c'était de voir de loin — mon regard blanc

to see this slope

to see it from afar

still alive

it was seeing from afar—my blank gaze

Part Two: *The Uninhabited*

[Poems from *In the Vacant Heat* and *Where the Sun*]

translated by Paul Auster

DU BORD DE LA FAUX

I

L'aridité qui découvre le jour.

De long en large, pendant que l'orage va de long en large.

Sur une voie qui demeure sèche malgré la pluie.

La terre immense se déverse, et rien n'est perdu.

A la déchirure dans le ciel, l'épaisseur du sol.

J'anime le lien des routes.

FROM THE EDGE OF THE SCYTHE

I

The dryness that discovers the day.

To and fro, as the storm goes to and fro.

On a path that stays dry in spite of the rain.

The immense earth spills, and nothing is lost.

For a rift in the sky, the strength of the soil.

I quicken the bond of roads.

II

La montagne,
                    la terre bue par le jour, sans
        que le mur bouge.

                La montagne
                comme une faille dans le souffle

                le corps du glacier.

Les nuées volant bas, au ras de la route,
        illuminant le papier.

Je ne parle pas avant ce ciel,
                            la déchirure,
                                        comme
        une maison rendue au souffle.

II

The mountain,
                the earth drunk by the day, without
        the wall moving.

                The mountain
                like a fault in the breath

                the body of the glacier.

The clouds flying low, level with the road,
    lighting the paper.

I do not speak before this sky,
                        the rift,
                                like
    a house given back to breath.

J'ai vu le jour ébranlé, sans que le mur bouge.

I saw the day shaken, and the wall never moved.

III

Le jour écorche les chevilles.

Veillant, volets tirés, dans la blancheur de la
pièce.

La blancheur des choses apparaît tard.

Je vais droit au jour turbulent.

III

The day rubs the ankles raw.

Keeping watch, shutters closed, in the whiteness of the room.

The whiteness of things comes out late.

I go straight into the eddying day.

LAPS

L'ombre,

      plus courte, la chaleur, dehors, nous

tenant lieu de feu. Rien ne nous sépare de la

chaleur. Sur le sol du foyer où j'avance,

                rompu,

   vers ces murs froids.

LAPSE

The shadow,

        shorter, the warmth, outside, replacing fire for us.

Nothing severs us from the warmth. On the hearth-ground,

through which I move,

           broken,

      toward these cold walls.

MÉTÉORE

L'absence qui me tient lieu de souffle recommence à tomber sur les papiers comme de la neige. La nuit apparaît. J'écris aussi loin que possible de moi.

METEOR

The absence that takes the place of breath in me begins to fall like snow on the papers again. The night appears. I write as far away from myself as possible.

ACCIDENTS

J'ai erré autour de cette lueur.

Je me suis déchiré, une nouvelle fois, de l'autre côté de ce mur, comme l'air que tu vois,

à cette lueur froide.

De l'autre côté du mur, je vois le même air aveuglant.

Dans le lointain sans rupture, comme l'étendue même de la terre entrecoupée que, plus loin, je foule, nul ne sent la chaleur.

Nous serons lavés de notre visage, comme l'air qui couronne le mur.

ACCIDENTS

I wandered around this glow.

                  I was torn, once again, from the other side of this wall, like the air you see,

                        in this cold glow. From the other side of the wall, I see the same blinding air.

                In the unbreached distance, like this stretch of broken earth, up ahead, I walk on, no one feels the heat.

We will be washed of our face, like the air that crowns the wall.

LE MOTEUR BLANC

I

J'ai vite enlevé
cette espèce de pansement arbitraire

je me suis retrouvé
libre
et sans espoir

comme un fagot
ou une pierre

je rayonne

avec la chaleur de la pierre

THE WHITE MOTOR

I

I quickly removed
this arbitrary bandage

I found myself
free
and without hope

like a bundle of sticks
or a stone

I radiate

with the heat of stone

qui ressemble à du froid
contre le corps du champ
mais je connais la chaleur et le froid

la membrure du feu

le feu

dont je vois
la tête

les membres blancs.

which resembles the cold
against the body of the field
but I know the heat and the cold

the framework of the fire

the fire

in which I see
the head

the white limbs.

II

Le feu perce en plusieurs points le côté sourd du ciel, le côté
que je n'avais jamais vu.

Le ciel qui se hisse un peu au-dessus de la terre. Le front noir.
Je ne sais pas si je suis ici ou là,
                              dans l'air ou dans l'ornière. Ce
sont des morceaux d'air que je foule comme des mottes.

Ma vie s'arrête avec le mur ou se met en marche là où le mur
s'arrête, au ciel éclaté. Je ne cesse pas.

II

At several points the fire pierces the sky, the deaf side, which I have never seen.

The sky that heaves a bit above the earth. The black brow. I don't know if I am here or there,

in the air or in a rut. They are scraps of air, which I crush like clumps of earth.

My life stops with the wall, or begins to walk where the wall stops, in the shattered sky. I do not stop.

III

Mon récit sera la branche noire qui fait un coude dans le ciel.

III

My telling will be the black branch that forms an elbow in the sky.

IV

Ici, il ouvre sa bouche blanche. Là, il se défend sur toute la ligne, avec ces arbres retranchés, ces êtres noirs. Là encore, il prend la forme lourde et chaude de la fatigue, comme des membres de terre écorchés par une charrue.

Je m'arrête au bord de mon souffle, comme d'une porte, pour écouter son cri.

Ici, dehors, il y a sur nous une main, un océan lourd et froid, comme si on accompagnait les pierres.

IV

Here, its white mouth opens. There, it defends itself along the whole line, with these entrenched trees, these black beings. There again, it takes the hot, heavy form of fatigue, like limbs of earth flayed by a plow.

I stop at the edge of my breath, as if beside a door, to listen to its cry.

Here, outside, a hand is upon us, a cold, heavy sea, as if, as the stones walk, we were walking with the stones.

V

Je sors
dans la chambre

comme si j'étais dehors

parmi des meubles
immobiles

dans la chaleur qui tremble

toute seule

hors de son feu

il n'y a toujours
rien

le vent.

V

I go out
inside the room

as if I were outside

among the motionless
furniture

in the shuddering heat

all alone

beyond its fire

there is not yet
anything

the wind.

VI

Je marche, réuni au feu, dans le papier vague confondu avec l'air, la terre désamorcée. Je prête mon bras au vent.

Je ne vais pas plus loin que mon papier. Très loin au-devant de moi, il comble un ravin. Un peu plus loin dans le champ, nous sommes presque à égalité. A mi-genoux dans les pierres.

A côté, on parle de plaie, on parle d'un arbre. Je me reconnais. Pour ne pas être fou. Pour que mes yeux ne deviennent pas aussi faibles que la terre.

VI

I walk, joined with fire, in the uncertain paper mingled with air, the unprimed earth. I lend my arm to the wind.

I go no farther than my paper. Far before me, it fills a ravine. A bit farther, in the field, we are almost level. Knee-deep in stones.

Nearby they speak of wounds, of a tree. I see myself in what they say. That I not be mad. That my eyes not become as weak as the earth.

VII

Je suis dans le champ
comme une goutte d'eau
sur du fer rouge

lui-même s'éclipse

les pierres s'ouvrent

comme une pile d'assiettes
que l'on tient
dans ses bras

quand le soir souffle

je reste
avec ces assiettes blanches et froides

VII

I am in the field
like a drop of water
on a red-hot iron

the field
eclipses itself

the stones open

like a stack of plates
held
in the arms

when evening breathes

I stay
with these cold white plates

comme si je tenais la terre
elle-même

dans mes bras.

as if I held the earth
itself

in my arms.

VIII

Déjà des araignées courent sur moi, sur la terre démembrée.
Je me lève droit au-dessus des labours, sur les vagues courtes
et sèches,
                              d'un champ accompli et devenu bleu,
où je marche sans facilité.

VIII

Already spiders are running over me, on the dismembered
earth. I rise above the plowing, on the clipped and arid runnels,
                              of a finished field, now blue, where I
stumble ahead.

IX

Rien ne me suffit. Je ne suffis à rien. Le feu qui souffle sera le fruit de ce jour-là, sur la route en fusion qui réussit à devenir blanche aux yeux heurtés des pierres.

IX

Nothing satisfies me. I satisfy nothing. The bellowing fire will be the fruit of that day, on the melding road, reaching whiteness in the battered eyes of stones.

X

Je freine pour apercevoir le champ vide, le ciel au-dessus du mur. Entre l'air et la pierre, j'entre dans un champ sans mur. Je sens la peau de l'air, et pourtant nous demeurons séparés.

Hors de nous, il n'y a pas de feu.

X

I brake to see the vacant field, the sky above the wall. Between
air and stone, I enter an unwalled field. I feel the skin of the air,
and yet we remain divided.

Beyond us, there is no fire.

XI

Une grande page blanche palpitante dans la lumière dévas-
tée dure jusqu'à ce que nous nous rapprochions.

XI

A large white page palpitating in the ruined light lasts until we get closer to each another.

XII

En lâchant la porte chaude, la poignée de fer, je me trouve devant un bruit qui n'a pas de fin, un tracteur. Je touche le fond d'un lit rugueux, je ne commence pas. J'ai toujours vécu. Je vois plus nettement les pierres, surtout l'ombre qui sertit, l'ombre rouge de la terre sur les doigts quand elle est fragile, sous ses tentures, et que la chaleur ne nous a pas cachés.

XII

In releasing the warm door, the iron knob, I find myself before a noise that has no end, a tractor. I touch the base of a gnarled bed, I do not begin. I have always lived. I see the stones more clearly—above all, the enclosing shadow, the earth's red shadow on my fingers when the earth is fragile, beneath its draping, which the heat has not hidden from us.

XIII

Ce feu, comme un mur plus lisse en prolongement vertical de l'autre et violemment heurté jusqu'au faîte où il nous aveugle, comme un mur que je ne laisse pas se pétrifier.

La terre relève sa tête sévère.

Ce feu comme une main ouverte auquel je renonce à donner un nom. Si la réalité est venue entre nous comme un coin et nous a séparés, c'est que j'étais trop près de cette chaleur, de ce feu.

XIII

This fire, like a smoother wall built on top of another, and struck violently up to its peak, where it blinds us like a wall I do not allow to turn to stone.

The earth lifts its harsh head.

The fire, like an open hand which I no longer wish to name. If reality has come between us like a wedge and divided us, it was because I was too close to this heat, to this fire.

XIV

Alors, tu as vu ces éclats de vent, ces grands disques de pain rompu, dans le pays brun, comme un marteau hors de sa gangue qui nage contre le courant sans rides dont on n'aperçoit que le lit rugueux, la route.

Ces fins éclats, ces grandes lames déposées par le vent.

Les pierres dressées, l'herbe à genoux. Et ce que je ne connais pas de profil et de dos, dès qu'il se tait : toi, comme la nuit.

Tu t'éloignes.

Ce feu dételé, ce feu qui n'est pas épuisé et qui nous embrase, comme un arbre, le long du talus.

XIV

So, you have seen these bursts of wind, these great discs of broken bread, in this brown country, like a hammer freed of its dross that swims against the unrippled current, of which nothing can be seen but the gnarled bed, the road.

These keening bursts, these great blades left by the wind.

The raised stones, the grass on its knees. What I don't know of the back and the profile, since the moment of soundlessness: you, like the night.

You recede.

This unharnessed fire, this unconsumed fire igniting us like a tree along the slope.

XV

Ce qui demeure après le feu, ce sont les pierres disqualifiées, les pierres froides, la monnaie de cendre dans le champ.

Il y a encore la carrosserie de l'écume qui cliquette comme si elle rejaillissait de l'arbre ancré dans la terre aux ongles cassés, cette tête qui émerge et s'ordonne, et le silence qui nous réclame comme un grand champ.

XV

What remains after the fire are disqualified stones, frigid stones, ashen coins in the field.

The carriage of the foam still remains, rattling, as if it had rushed forth again from the tree anchored to the earth with broken nails, this head that emerges and falls into place, and the silence that claims us, like a vast field.

CE QUE LA LAMPE A BRULÉ

Comme une plaie qui se répète

la lumière

où nous enfonçons

l'ombre
estimée par la montagne
la hauteur de l'ombre

j'ai commencé
par être

cette mèche défaite

la terre

WHAT THE LAMP BURNED

Like a wound
again and again

the light

in which we sink

shadow
sized up by the mountain
the height of the shadow

I began
by being

this tousled fuse

the earth

où passe
la manche du vent.

where the sleeve of the wind
is passing.

Je me dissipe sans renoncer à mon feu,

                                        sur une pente

droite.

        De pierre. Aujourd'hui ma bouche est neuve. Au bout de la descente, je recommence.

Comme un plafond qu'on regarde dans un miroir, je réunis les reflets de la montagne.

La lumière est dans la partie noire de la pièce, dans le coin sombre où la table se soulève.

Un chemin, comme un torrent sans souffle. Je prête mon souffle aux pierres. J'avance, avec de l'ombre sur les épaules.

I dissipate, without renouncing my fire,

                         on a straight

slope.

        Of stone. Today my mouth is new. After I finish climb-
ing down, I start up again.

Like a ceiling that is watched in a mirror, I unite the reflections
of the mountain.

The light is in the black part of the room, in the dimmed corner
where the table heaves.

A path, like a torrent without breath. I lend my breath to the
stones. I move on, with shadows on my shoulders.

Nous nous reconnaissons à notre fatigue, le bois des membres, le bûcher tout à coup délaissé par le feu, et froid au fond du jour. Nous prenons froid. Puis j'ai tourné le dos à ceux qui s'embrassent.

Notre faux enjambe la campagne. Nous allons plus vite que les routes. Plus vite qu'une voiture. Aussi vite que le froid.

Déjà le pays perce. Je ne m'arrête pas. Je vois le chemin que nous n'avons pas pris à travers notre visage.

Quand je ne vois rien, je vois l'air. Je tiens le froid par les manches.

We recognize ourselves by our fatigue, the wood of limbs, the pyre suddenly abandoned by the flame, and cold at the bottom of the day. We shudder in the cold. Then I turned my back on those who embrace.

Our scythe straddles the country. We go faster than the roads. Faster than a car. As fast as the cold.

Already the country pierces. I do not stop. Through our face I see the path we did not take.

When I see nothing, I see the air. I grasp the cold by its handles.

CESSION

Le vent,
   dans les terres sans eau de l'été, nous
      quitte sur une lame,
         ce qui subsiste du ciel.

En plusieurs fractures, la terre se précise. La terre demeure stable dans le souffle qui nous dénude.

Ici, dans le monde immobile et bleu, j'ai presque atteint ce mur. Le fond du jour est encore devant nous. Le fond embrasé de la terre. Le fond et la surface du front,
      aplani par le même souffle,
ce froid.

Je me recompose au pied de la façade comme l'air bleu au pied des labours.

       Rien ne désaltère mon pas.

GIVING OVER

The wind,
      in the waterless lands of summer, leaves us
            on a blade,
                  what is left of the sky.

The earth defines itself in several fissures. The earth endures, equal to itself, in the breath that strips us bare.

Here, in the blue and motionless world, I have almost reached this wall. The bottom of the day is still ahead of us. The bottom of ignited earth. The bottom and the surface of the forehead,
      leveled by the same breath,
this cold.

I gather myself anew at the foot of this facade like the blue air at the foot of the plowing.

                  Nothing quenches my step.

OÙ LE SOLEIL

Où le soleil
— le disque froid de la terre, le disque noir et piétiné,
où le soleil a disparu — jusqu'à l'air, plus haut, que
nous n'habiterons pas.

WHERE THE SUN

Where the sun
— the cold, earthen disc, the black and trodden disc,
where the sun disappeared — upward, into the air
we shall not inhabit.

Sombrant, comme le soleil,
que nous ayons disparu — le travail du soleil — ou avancé
encore.

Jusqu'à nous — chemin raboteux au front.

J'ai couru avec le soleil qui disparaît.

                              Sinking, like the sun,
whether we have disappeared — the work of the sun — or
again moving on.

                    Up to us — rugged road up to the brow.

                    I ran with the sun that disappeared.

                              ·

Lumière, j'ai eu pied.

Jusqu'à l'air que nous ne respirons
pas — jusqu'à nous.

Demain — déjà, comme un nœud
dans le jour. Le vent arrêté retentit.

Light, I've held my ground.

Up to the air we do not

breathe — up to us.

Tomorrow — already,

like a knot in the day. The halted wind thunders.

Comme, au-dessous de la figure
de l'air
        épars, dans les terres sur elle retournées, paille, elle,
que le vent cherche, toujours —

S'arrache, comme j'avance — s'arrache à ses lointains,
le nouveau sol ajouré.

As, under the figure
of the sparse
                    air, in soils overturned upon it, straw, it,
sought by the wind, still —

Uprooting itself, as I move on — uprooted
from its distances, the new soil, shot through with light.

Jusqu'à ce sol habité sous le pas,
qui tarit — sous le pas seulement.

Comme le regard
de ce que je n'ai pas vu — et en avant.

Sous le pas, seulement, accueillant au jour.

Up to this earth inhabited under the step,
that dries up — only under the step.

Like the look
of what I have not seen — ahead as well.

Under the step, only, opening up to the day.

La face d'eau des glaciers. La face d'eau debout dans le jour.

Mais la terre, comme je cours encore, est arrêtée au-dessous du vent.

Par les pierres des chemins sans eau. Les pierres à moitié —

The face of water from the glaciers. The face of water standing
in the day.

                                    But the earth, as long as I run,
is stopped under the wind.

Through the stones of waterless paths. Stones half-way —

Dans le jour en poudre,
et du même pas — sur nous, froid, et souffle, comme
en suspens.

A travers ce que donne, au loin, une foulée encore (fardeau
masquant le feu,
                    la fraîcheur)

L'air —
sans atteindre au sol, seulement — sous la foulée, revient.

                              In the day and its dust,
with the same step — upon us, cold, and breath, as if
hovering.

Through what gives, in the distance, another step (a burden
masking the fire,
                   the coolness)

                                        The air —
without reaching the soil, even — under the step, returns.

L'INHABITÉ

Nous nous arrêterons,
pour la hauteur, dans le vent qui n'assèche pas les lointains,
sur l'empierrement debout.

Notre appui souffle. Le ciel est comble,

et s'ouvre encore.

THE UNINHABITED

We will stop,
because of the height, in the wind that does not dry up
    distances,
on the stone-work standing.

Our support is heaving. The sky is full,

and opening again.

LES JALONS

                    L'un sur l'autre fermés —
comme, autour du pas enfoui, le soleil,
                    courte terre.

                    Le soleil, encore,
        le soleil, autour de ce pas, résonne.

MARKING POSTS

Each closed upon the other —
as, around the buried step, the sun,

short-lived earth.

The sun, still,
the sun, around this step, reverberates.

Le vestige du pas du soleil. Entre nous. Entre soleil et nous.

Comme la terre, alors, sur laquelle aura passé — plus loin, je la vois — le soleil.

The vestige of the sun's step. Between
us. Between sun and us.

Like the earth, then,
on which will have passed — farther, I see it — the sun.

Paille dans l'épaisseur, sur l'affût

d'un souffle

qui coupe, l'éclat !

Jusqu'à ce lointain qu'elle emporte, elle,
dans le jour. Comme je te rejoins.

Mais le vestige est en avant.

S'interrompt, comme je te rejoins, où le jour aura fusé.

Straw in the thickness, on the whetstone

of a breath

that cuts, the slice!

Up to this distance it carries, it,

in the day. As I reach you.

But the remains are still ahead of us.

Interrupted, as I meet you, where the day will have fused.

ASSIETTE

Agrandi jusqu'au blanc

l'époque
le morceau de terre
où je glisse

comme rayonnant de froid

dans le jour cahotant.

PLAIN

Grown until white

the age
the piece of earth
where I slip

as if radiating from cold

in the jolting day.

Quand je dis charbon
je veux dire
hiver

c'est ce qu'il avait voulu dire
par cette bourrasque

la toux

les contusions

tout est posé comme une blessure

When I say coal
I want to say
winter

what it would have wanted to say
through this squall

the cough

contusions

everything set like a wound

l'assiette immobile

les objets nés des mains
s'ouvrent
                    au fond de l'air

                    cuisant.

the motionless plate

objects born from the hands
open
                    at the bottom of the air

                    burning.

Ébréché
par un tombereau

l'air bleu

partout où mon front
trouve

la terre

ou le front de la terre.

Chipped
by a tip-cart

the blue air

everywhere my forehead
finds

the earth

or the forehead of the earth.

Dans une chambre
froide
de loin dorée

la lumière est un pli

je la vois
sans sombrer

presque sous les roues

comme le mûrier
que la route blanchit.

In a cold
room
gilded from afar

the light is a fold

I see it
without sinking

almost under the wheels

like the mulberry
the road whitens.

AJOURNEMENT

J'occupe seul cette demeure
blanche

où rien ne contrarie le vent

si nous sommes ce qui a crié
et le cri

qui ouvre ce ciel
de glace

ce plafond blanc

nous nous sommes aimés sous ce plafond.

POSTPONEMENT

Alone I inhabit this white
place

where nothing thwarts the wind

if we are what cried
and the cry

that opens this sky
of ice

this white ceiling

we have loved under this ceiling.

Je vois presque,
à la blancheur de l'orage, ce qui se fera sans moi.

Je ne diminue pas. Je respire au pied de la lumière aride.

I almost see,
in the whiteness of the storm, what will come to pass without
me.

I do not diminish. I breathe at the foot of arid light.

S'il n'y avait pas la force
de la poussière
qui coupe jambes et bras

mais seul le blanc
qui verse

je tiendrais le ciel

profonde ornière
avec laquelle nous tournons

et qui donne contre l'air.

If there were not the force
of dust
that severs arms and legs

but only the white
that spills

I would hold the sky

deep rut
with which we turn

and which knocks against the air.

Dans cette lumière que le soleil
abandonne, toute chaleur résolue en feu, j'ai couru, cloué
à la lumière des routes, jusqu'à ce que le vent plie.

Où je déchire l'air,

tu as passé avec moi. Je te retrouve
dans la chaleur. Dans l'air, encore plus loin, qui s'arrache,
d'une secousse, à la chaleur.

La poussière illumine. La montagne,
faible lampe, apparaît.

In this light the sun
abandons, all heat resolved in fire, I ran, nailed to the light
of roads, till the wind buckled under.

Where I split the air,
you have come through with me. I find you
in the heat. In the air, even farther, which uproots itself,
with a single jolt, away from the heat.

The dust lights up. The mountain,
frail lamp, appears.

LA LUMIÈRE DE LA LAME

Ce glacier qui grince

pour dire
la fraîcheur de la terre

sans respirer.

THE LIGHT OF THE BLADE

This glacier that creaks

to utter
the cool of earth

without breathing.

Comme du papier à plat sur cette terre,
ou un peu au-dessus de la terre,
comme une lame je cesse
de respirer. La nuit je me retourne, un instant, pour le dire.

À la place de l'arbre.
À la clarté des pierres.

J'ai vu, tout le long du jour,
la poutre sombre et bleue qui barre le jour se soulever
pour nous rejoindre dans la lumière immobile.

Like paper flat against this earth,
or a bit above the earth,
like a blade I stop breathing. At night
I return to myself, for a moment, to utter it.

In the place of the tree.
In the light of the stones.

I saw, all along the day,
the dark blue rafter that bars the day rise up to reach us
in the motionless light.

Je marche dans les éclats de la poussière
qui nous réfléchit.

Dans le souffle court
et bleu
      de l'air qui claque

loin du souffle

l'air tremble et claque.

                        I walk in the gleams of dust
that mirror us.

                In the short blue
                breath
                        of the clattering air

                far from breath

                the air trembles and clatters.

CETTE SURFACE

                              De la terre,
je ne connais que la surface.

                              Je l'ai embrassée.

THIS SURFACE

Of the earth,

I know nothing but the surface.

I have embraced it.

J'ai fait mon front
de cette destruction

le froid
l'été pivotent sur lui

du jour

ce mur élimé
comme une langue qui râpe

avant de tomber.

I have made my brow
out of this destruction

the cold
the summer revolving on it

from the day

this frayed wall
like a tongue that rasps

before it falls.

La lampe

est un feu froid,

puis le froid se révèle dans l'obscurité.

Pendant que des bouffées
de froid entrent dans la pièce, je suis encore en proie à cette
marche, je trouve de toutes parts la terre qui me précède et qui
me suit.

The lamp

is a cold fire,

then the cold comes out in the darkness.

While the gusts
of cold enter the room, I am still prey to this step, everywhere I
find the earth that comes before me and after me.

Plus chaude que moi, la paille qui enveloppe
notre pas venu de terre — notre pas comme cette clarté
dans le corps

de la terre.

Warmer than I, the straw that envelops
our step emerging from the earth — our step like this dawning
in the body

of earth.

BILLON

Fleurs dans l'air âpte et froid
sur nous retournées (j'ai vu leur pas de haut)

Comme par les routes le genou
plie,
l'air — plus lent, plus loin — soleil après le jour,
qui rompt le souffle.

Le front des montagnes rentre. La fraîcheur de la route
reprend.

PLOW-RIDGE

Flowers in the cold and rasping air
overturned upon us (I saw their step above)

As on the roads the knee
bends,
        the air — slower, farther — sun after the day,
that breaks the breath.

The brow of the mountains comes in again. The coolness
of the road revives.

Souffle
sur quoi le jour interrompu

comme glacier dans le jour

reprend.

Breath
on what the interrupted day

like a glacier in the day

revives.

Comme
au pied immobile
le sol sans attache

l'air.

As
under the motionless foot
the untethered ground

the air.

Au-dessus du front enfoui, courte houle, la terre foulée refer-
mée. La minceur de l'autre face — tant que l'air a soufflé —
entre soleil et nous.

S'est glissé. Entre nous s'est glissé. Le froid, alors, s'est
glissé.

Comme, sous le pas,
— tant que l'air a soufflé, entre soleil et nous, la mince terre.

Above the buried forehead, brief surge, the trodden earth again closed. The thinness of the other face — so thin that air can breathe — between sun and us.

Has slid. Between us has slid. The cold, then,
has slid.

As, under the step,
— so much that air can breathe, between sun and us, the thin earth.

Dehors

où, sur ce qui souffle,
la porte, après le vent, se sera fermée, l'air — où l'un de nous
a disparu. L'air après le vent.

Outside

                              where, upon what breathes,
the door, after the wind, will have shut, the air — where one
of us

has disappeared. Air after the wind.

De l'autre côté de cette face,
comme illuminera — de l'autre côté de la poussière,
le soleil

enfoui.

Qui parle sur l'air interrompu, le vent le serre. Le vent de loin
le serre.

On the other side of this face,
as it will light up — on the other side of the dust,

the buried

sun.

Whoever speaks on interrupted air, the wind clasps him. The
distant wind clasps him.

La terre avec le souffle
— entre soleil et nous — confondus. Mais le soleil qui
emporte
est pour moitié dans l'épaisseur.

Où,
jetés — l'un de nous, et l'autre — tu puises cette chaleur
qui heurte. Comme, à l'entour du sol de la terre fermée, en
avant
de nous,
notre souffle. Tout est à toi. Vient pour toi.

Le jour

comme, après soi, le jour.
L'armoise. La consoude
dans sa poudre.

Earth with breath
— between sun and us — merged. But the sun that bears
   away
is half in the thickness.

Where,
thrown — one of us, and the other — you draw up
this heat that knocks. As, around the soil of the shut earth,
   ahead
of us,
     our breath. Everything is yours. Is coming for you.

The day

as, after oneself, the day.
     The wormwood. The comfrey
           in its dust.

Part Three: Late Poems

translated by Hoyt Rogers

PEINTURE

              toutes les choses ont un air
d'attente, aussitôt qu'on les voit.   est-ce à la
              ressemblance avérée
que nous les saurons, en même temps que nous,
                   ici.

             elle-même, c'est
la réalité — autre, et qui ne ressemble à rien, que nous
désirons.   déjà, dans l'embrasure, elle fleurit.   dans
le halo d'une floraison au ras, qui perce à travers toute
apparence.   presque sans émoi.

                   .

le carreau.   les pampres
          de la façade.   dans
les branchages, le bris du ciel.   ainsi se fêle, et
fleurit, la fatigue, la fraîcheur du monde reçu.

PAINTING

all things look as if
they are waiting, as soon as we see them.   is it by their
proven resemblance
that we will know they are, at the same time that we are,
here.

itself, it is
reality — other, and resembling nothing, that we
desire.   already, in the doorway, it flowers.   in
the halo flush with bloom, which cuts through all
appearance.   almost unmoved.

the tile.   the vines
of the façade.   in
the branchings, the breakage of the sky. this is how the given world's
fatigue, its freshness, cracks and flowers.

il arrive
que, parvenus à cette chose même que nous avons désirée,
elle se perde dans une différence infinie.   nulle
illusion si la croisée renvoyant la couleur de sa lumière au
bleu qu'on ne voit pas, est pour jamais confondue avec
lui.   qui, alors, dira le nom des choses reconnues ?
déjà, dans cette attente, elles ont fleuri.

                                             it happens

that, once we have reached the thing we desired,

it may slip away into an infinite otherness.   no

illusion if the window returning the color of its light to the

blue we do not see, is forever merged with

that blue.   who, then, will say the name of recognized things?

already, through our waiting, they have flowered.

J'INTERLETTRE ...

terre,
au travers de mon sommeil, de nouveau entrevue sur
l'haleine, non l'ébruitement, de ce mot.

... étrécie
à un souffle sans lequel je ne peux pas articuler. moindre
souffle ne suffit pas.

•

grandes enjambées de l'herbe dans les près.

I INTERLETTER . . .

earth,

straddling my sleep, glimpsed again on
the breath, not the sound, of this word.

. . . shrunken

to a breath without which I cannot say it.   less
breath would not be enough.

•

big strides of grass in the meadows.

           ... malgré soi

en avant.   aujourd'hui, sur la parole en avant.   à

           l'orée.

      •

un, tout à coup, et quelques-uns.   échelonnés selon le degré de la vélocité ou du retard avec lequel ils gagnent le foyer aveuglant.   le dernier n'est pas loin, encore que j'aie autant de peine, dans mon opacité, à le distinguer du plus prompt qui, en avant lui-même, a presque disparu.

... ici, à toutes jambes.   à vue d'œil, là.

      courant

sur le soleil.   sur ce qui sépare encore de la disparition du soleil.

                                          . . . despite yourself
ahead.   today, with the word moving ahead.   at
                                          the verge.

                          •

one, all of sudden, and several.   whether swift or slow they
strive to reach the blinding hearth.   the last isn't far, though
blocked from my view and as hard to pick it out as the fastest,
which is ahead and has almost disappeared.

. . . here, as fast as your legs can carry you.   before your eyes, there.

                                          running
on the sun.   on what postpones the disappearance
of the sun.

le course supplée.   les jambes suppléent au jour.

the race is all.   legs replace the day.

LE RÉVOLU

De face, comme au sol
révolu, je vois la roue de face comme rentrée, qui ramène
sans dévier à des yeux qu'on racle.

pour en finir avec la route où les chemins déversent,
avec l'air aussi, pur plissement ...

l'atelier des torrents, le glacier, avance dans le rêche.

aussi râpeux,
rugueux, que le bleu dans notre bouche, le bleu qui ne
voit pas.

BYGONE

Head-on, as if on the ground
of long ago, I see the wheel come back, head-on, unswerving,
returning to eyes scraped clean.

to finish with the road where paths spill down,
finish as well with the pure creasing of the air . . .

the workshop of torrents, the glacier, plows through the roughness.

as rasping,
as rugged as the blue in our mouth, the blue that
does not see.

dans l'emportement de la soif,
nos têtes, et la montagne, obstruent.

il y a — aussi loin que nous aurons
été — ce visage soustrait qui tire à soi comme un long
trait d'eau froide.

même âge, j'ai crié
pour chaque herbe grandie.   La couverture râpeuse de
l'autre souffle tire.

when we are swept away by thirst,
our heads, and the mountain, block our way.

there is — as far-off as we have ever
been — this withheld face, which draws itself a long
drink of cold water.

same age, I gasped
as each grass-blade grew.   The rough blanket of
the other breath draws us in.

ici sans paroi,

comme derrière le bandeau des murs

le soleil rugueux,

illumine.

des mains vont,

la nuit, comme à l'eau.   vont, comme l'eau.   comme,

de l'autre côté des murs, le murmure, encore, de l'eau.

                                        here without a barrier,
                            as behind the blindfold of the walls
the rugged sun,

                                                brightens.

                                                    hands go,
at night, as to water.   go, as to water.   as,
on the far side of the walls, again, the murmuring of water.

•

Toi, dans la confusion des torrents, toi sans gangue !

•

Feu

pour brûler uniquement

donner flamme
fendue.

•

You, in the mayhem of the torrents, purified at last!

•

Fire

for burning only

to give
a split flame.

ÉCLAT

J'étais éclat : tu me l'as dit.   sur la fin de
l'autre jour, tes lèvres m'auront dit
                                              éclat.

FLASH OF LIGHT

I was a flash of light: you told me so.   at the end of
the other day, your lips called me
                                                   a flash of light.

... dans le jour,

éclat

du jour.   chaque éclat étant, dans l'amas des montagnes
— qui inhume, pommette de la face tournée vers l'air
et venant à moi ...

sous les yeux.   sous les yeux.

... je rejoins — comme je m'y pulvérise — l'épaisseur
où tu m'as dit éclat.

comme, l'autre jour, sur sa soif le jour.

         . . . in the day,

           a burst

of daylight. each flash, buried in the scumble of mountains
— is a cheekbone of the face turned toward the air
coming at me . . .

    before our eyes.   before our eyes.

. . . I go back — for there I turn to dust — back to the denseness
where you called me a flash of light.

    as, the other day, the daylight's thirst.

... dans le jour, l'éclat
du jour.

à son épaisseur je me confonds, où, tranchant
étendu au plat de sa lame, tu me l'avais dit.

                           . . . in the day, the flash
of daylight.
        I merge with its denseness where, a cutting-edge
laid flat on its blade, you said that to me.

SOUTIRÉ À UN FUTUR

déjà,

toi qui à tes pieds as pu porter
la terre, tu sais — avant de te voir, glacier rétractile,
en sens inverse vaporisé, qu'ici, et plus avant, de nouveau
elle s'aggravera.

éventé — comme debout
et hors du vent.

WITHDRAWN FROM A FUTURE

already,

        backward-moving glacier, who have been able
to carry the earth at your feet, you know—before seeing yourself
dissolve in reverse, that here, and farther on, once again the ground
will weigh more heavily.

        shouted to the winds—as if standing up
and outside the wind.

sur l'entoilure de l'air qui
tonne, la main assujettie aux lèvres n'a pas inscrit.

montagne calmée par l'eau à quai.

la passion
des hirondelles : neige — à une extrémité faite cri,
qu'à nouveau l'hirondelle carde.

cœur du glacier, le point de nouveau à quoi se voir
soudé.

                    on the canvas of thundering
air, the hand tamed by lips has inscribed nothing.

mountain becalmed by docked water.

                                     the passion
of swallows: snow — at one extreme turned into a cry
the swallow combs again.

heart of the glacier, the point on which we are
welded again.

                                             récitation sur les
        éclats de glace.   lumière
              intouchée de nouveau arrachée
                           aujourd'hui, et à l'arrét.

  recitation

on glints of ice.   untouched

                light ripped out again

                          today, at a standstill.

et, dans le froid de l'air, comme
on s'immobilise, pourvoir à une face de nouveau.   dans
cette face, la montagne sera rentrée.
de nouveau j'appose
à la face la montagne.

sur la pierre les yeux cassés
sont vivants.

and, in the chill of air, how
we stop in our tracks, divining yet another face.   into
this face, the mountain has pulled back.

again I affix
the mountain to the face.

on the stone the broken eyes
are alive.

CRÈTE

... Byzance
dans le caillou

pourvu que l'ongle incarné
y

bute.

CRETE

    . . . Byzantium
in this rock

as long as the incarnate
toe

is stubbed.

    ... ne voulant pas aciérer l'eau
des eaux.

    ... et
            jambes pendantes
    dans l'instant

    que ce jour
    a

    creusé.

. . . not wanting to turn the water of waters

to steel.

. . . and
        legs dangling
into the moment

this day
has

dug.

                    ... monde
        soustrait à monde

        tu es
        là

        comme sur sa hampe l'eau.

. . . world

withdrawn from world

you are
there

like falling water.

           ... dos
à la montagne
               sans être
à elle adossé

comme
entre moi et monde.

      . . . your back
to the mountain
          without leaning
back on the mountain

as between
me and the world.

... à
avoir

tu puises

comme avoir
été.

. . . you

draw

on having

as though on having
been.

... face

                          de part

en
part

à
la porte ouverte.

. . . looking

       all

the way
through

the open
door.

partir, alors, comme la neige.   sans voir et
                                    sans bruit.

to leave, then, like the snow.   without seeing
                without sound.

PIERRE OU EAU

           ... en avant
du centre
           serré
comme pierre un instant

ou eau.

STONE OR WATER

           . . . ahead
of the center
          gripped
like stone for an instant

or water.

                              ... l'oubli
          au centre
          où
                pierre
          un instant ou eau

          a été serrée.

                                        ... et immobile
          après le centre.

. . . oblivion

at the center

where

stone

for an instant or water

has been gripped.

. . . and motionless

after the center.

... le cœur de la montagne sera pierre

ou eau.

. . . the heart of the mountain will be stone

or water.

CÉLÉRITÉ

                                                    ... ralentir.
        montagne, je le dois.

                                                    ce sera.

                                comme — et sans qu'il y ait
        eu butoir — avoir heurté, soi

SWIFTNESS

. . . slow down.

mountain, I must.

it will be.

as if — and without any stumbling
block — we had bumped into our own

confondu.

ralentir.

confusion.

slow down.

... à travers feuilles
trémières
comme
                    hier

un instant
et

les rêches.

. . . through leaves
hollyhocks
as if
      yesterday

through and through
riddled

rough.

SANG

... sang

tel qu'

                              est

pour le dire
de surcroît
          accouru sourdre
un mot

le mot est là

pas moi.

BLOOD

. . . blood

such is

                    the way
a word
to over-
state it
        rushes to well up

the word is there

not I.

PEINTURE

après la porte, je
suis — et ouvert, dans ce què j'ai ouvert.

où la couleur
n'a été qu'écharde de la couleur, sans doute tient-elle
moins de la couleur même qu'à travers cette couleur
d'une écharde encore, et
comme elle perce, froide et d'avant la couleur.

sa percée,
c'est ce qui de l'identité perdue
comme la porte un peu plus loin
debout quand elle s'ouvre fera saillie.

PAINTING

after the door, I
am — and open, in what I have opened.

where color
has been just a splinter of color, no doubt it is less
like the color itself than still a splinter
through that color, and
since it pierces, it looms coldly in front of the color.

its piercing,
like the door ahead
when it opens, that is what it will project
from the loss of identity.

tout le reste de la personne

à échéance suit.

all the rest of the person

must then follow suit.

œil et la
main — en avant de soi, ouvre une étendue où le
reste de la personne
a disparu.

l'impersonnel
scindé.

œil touchant — comme écharde — le point
sensible où de nouveau tu as fui.

the eye and the

hand — in front of us, open an expanse where the
rest of the person

has disappeared.

the impersonal

split apart.

eye touching — like a splinter — the sensitive
point to which you have fled once again.

le futur — de retour sur
soi, éblouit.

the future — turning back

on itself, dazzles.

mais c'est toi, couleur, si tu te reconnais dans l'identité perdue, toi-même comme un regard aveuglément se pose où la main aveugle s'est posée.

but color is you, if you recognize yourself in
the identity you have lost, yourself like a look that blindly
rests where the blind hand rests.

D'UN CARNET

quelque chose de l'épaisseur du
vent comme il a pris se dérobe à soi.

ardoise poursuivie sur la lancée
de sa compression.

FROM A NOTEBOOK

                                something of the thickness
of the wind when it starts to blow steals away from itself.

                                slate pursued in the vein
of its compression.

soif

abouchée à la soif traverse la barrière.

je n'ai trouvé montagne que dans l'arrachement.

  thirst

entwined with thirst crosses the barrier.

I have found mountain only by tearing it out.

que tu me parviennes, neige, comme — à travers la brûlure
ou des carreaux, l'homme allongeant le pas dans la neige.

ici j'ai gardé contact avec le froid.

may you reach me, snow, as — across scalding
or tiles a man hurries his step in the snow.

here I have kept in touch with the cold.

image, je l'ai cherchée à sa
racine — la disparition.

froid sur lequel j'ai, une fois, respiré.   cela n'est
qu'une fois, alors même qu'à l'infini
recommencé.

image, I have sought it at its

root — disappearance.

cold on which I've breathed, once.   that is

only once, though endlessly

begun again.

                                        récurrence,
ou un cillement — l'épaisseur.

                                    le ciel entre paupière et
soi, je n'ai pas — sinon pour le solidifier,
                                        à le rapporter à la
            cassure.

lavandes, bleu enfermé.

                            Il a suffi — pour enfouir l'image
adventice, de lever la tête.

                      recurrence,

or a blinking — the thickness.

                    unless to make it solid,

I do not need to — break the sky

                    between eyelid

       and self.

bushes of lavender, locked-up blue.

          It was enough — so as to bury the self-born

image, to lift my head.

comme

est le sol où mon pied a eu place.

épongée la poussière qui
a donné le bleu, la terre ronde est devenue noire.

la couleur a percé.

air porteur
de la parole disparue.

as

is the ground where my foot has found room.

the dust that gave blueness
sponged away, the round earth has turned black.

color has broken through.

air that carries
vanished words.

enclume ici et là qui prononcera les distances.   air
porteur.   enclume disparue.

parole — enclume disparue — comme incluse.

une coulée — signe de l'escarpement.

the anvil here and there which will speak of distances.   air
that bears.   vanished anvil.

words — vanished anvil — as gone together.

a mudslide — sign of the steep slope.

montagne
allégée de son faîte, et sur ses à-plats de nouveau soustraite
à une image impraticable.

montagne restée la face dans laquelle déjà s'apercevoir
des pieds à la tête
engagé.

sommités fleuries
où sur son demi-tour le ciel circulaire à nouveau fiché.

trancher
sans conclure.

ce qui demeure soustrait, c'est la terre qu'ici on aura croisée.

mountain

shorn of its summit, and on its ledges once again removed
from an unworkable image.

mountain,   the   perception   of   that   face
already from head to foot
still engaging us.

eminences, flowered heights
where the circular sun has turned around to stake its claim again.

cut to the chase

make no conclusions.

what remains removed is the earth we will have crossed.

　　　　　　　　　　... jusqu'à l'ouverture de ce demi-tour
qui dans l'épaisseur — là où l'épaisseur a refait surface —
　　　　　　　　　　　　　　　　　　me reconduit à moi
　　　où je dois terminer.

. . . an about-face
in the thick of things — where new surfaces are found —
this brings me back to myself
where I must end.

Preface to *The Uninhabited*

> . . . this irreducible sign — *deutungslos* — . . . a word beyond
> grasping, Cassandra's word, a word from which no lesson
> is to be drawn, a word, each time, and every time,
> spoken to say nothing . . .
> — *Hölderlin aujourd'hui* (lecture delivered March 1970 in Stuttgart
> to commemorate the 200th anniversary of Hölderlin's birth)

> (this joy . . . that is born of nothing . . .)
> — *Qui n'est pas tourné vers nous* (1972)

Born of the deepest silences, and condemned to life without hope
of life (*I found myself / free / and without hope*), the poetry of André
du Bouchet stands, in the end, as an act of survival. Beginning with
nothing, and ending with nothing but the truth of its own struggle,
du Bouchet's work is the record of an obsessive, wholly ruthless at-
tempt to gain access to the self. It is a project filled with uncertainty,
silence, and resistance, and there is no contemporary poetry, per-
haps, that lends itself more reluctantly to gloss. To read du Bouchet
is to undergo a process of dislocation: here, we discover, is not here,
and the body, even the physical presence within the poems, is no
longer in possession of itself — but moving, as if into the distance,
where it seeks to find itself against the inevitability of its own disap-
pearance (*. . . and the silence that claims us, like a vast field*). "Here"

is the limit we come to. To be in the poem, from this moment on, is to be nowhere.

A body in space. And the poem, as self-evident as this body. In space: that is to say, this void, this nowhere between sky and earth, rediscovered with each step that is taken. For wherever we are, the world is not. And wherever we go, we find ourselves moving in advance of ourselves—as if where the world would be. The distance, which allows the world to appear, is also that which separates us from the world, and though the body will endlessly move through this space, as if in the hope of abolishing it, the process begins again with the hazarding of each new step. We move toward an infinitely receding point, a destination that can never be reached, and in the end, this going, in itself, will become a goal, so that the mere fact of moving onward will be a way of being in the world, even as the world remains beyond us. There is no hope in this, but neither is there despair. For what du Bouchet manages to maintain, almost uncannily, is a nostalgia for a possible future, even as he knows it will never come to pass. And from this dreadful knowledge, there is nevertheless a kind of joy, a joy . . . that is born of nothing.

Du Bouchet's work, however, will seem difficult to many readers approaching it for the first time. Stripped of metaphor, almost devoid of imagery, and generated by a syntax of abrupt, paratactic brevity, his poems have done away with nearly all the props that students of poetry are taught to look for—the very difficulties that poetry has always seemed to rely on—and this sudden opening of distances, in spite of the lessons buried in such earlier poets as Hölderlin, Leopardi, and Mallarmé, will seem baffling, even frightening. In the world of French poetry, however, du Bouchet has performed an act of linguistic surgery no less important than the one performed by William Carlos Williams in America, and against the rhetorical inflation that is the curse of French writing, his intensely understated poems have all the freshness of natural objects. His work, which was first published in the early fifties, became a model for a whole generation of post-war poets, and there are few young poets in France today who do not show the mark of his influence. What on first or second reading might seem to be an almost fragile sensibility gradually emerges as a vision of the greatest force and purity. For the poems themselves cannot be truly felt until one has penetrated the strength of the silence that lies at their source. It is a silence equal to the strength of any word.

— Paul Auster
Paris, 1973

SELECT BIBLIOGRAPHY

The listings are in chronological order, and in keeping with the cata-logue of the Bibliothèque Nationale de France. — HR

Works by André du Bouchet

Air. Paris: J. Aubier, 1951. [First version, 1946.]

Sans couvercle. Paris: G.L.M., 1953.

Dans la chaleur vacante. Paris: Mercure de France, 1961.

Où le soleil. Paris: Mercure de France, 1968.

Qui n'est pas tourné vers nous. Paris: Mercure de France, 1972.

Air: 1950–1953. Paris: Clivages, 1977.

Peinture. Saint-Clément-la-Rivière: Fata Morgana, 1983.

Laisses. Paris: Hachette, Paris, 1979. Reprint, Fata Morgana, 1984.

L'incohérence. Paris: Hachette, 1979. Reprint, Fata Morgana, 1984.

Rapides. Paris: Hachette, 1980. Reprint, Fata Morgana, 1984.

Aujourd'hui c'est. Fontfroide-le-Haut: Fata Morgana, 1984.

Air ; (suivi de) Défets : 1950–1953. Frontfroide-le-Haut: Fata Morgana, 1986.

Cendre tirant sur le bleu. Paris: Clivages, 1986.

Ici en deux. Paris: Mercure de France, 1986.

Une tache. Fontfroide-le-Haut: Fata Morgana, 1988.

Carnets, 1952–1956. Edited by Michel Collot. Paris: Plon, 1989.

De plusieurs déchirements dans les parages de la peinture. Le Muy: Éditions Unes, 1990.

Verses. Le Muy: Éditions Unes, 1990.

Alberto Giacometti, « Dessin ». Paris: Maeght, 1991.

Axiales. Paris: Mercure de France, 1992.

Matière de l'interlocuteur. Saint-Clément-la-Rivière: Fata Morgana, 1992.

Carnet [1950–1961]. Fontfroide-le-Haut: Fata Morgana, 1994.

Dans la chaleur vacante (suivi de) Ou le soleil. Paris: Poésie-Gallimard, 1995.

Poèmes et proses. Paris: Mercure de France, 1995.

Retours sur le vent. Paris: Éditions Fourbis, 1995.

Pourquoi si calmes. Saint-Clément: Fata Morgana, 1996.

D'un trait qui figure et défigure. Saint-Clément: Fata Morgana, 1997.

Carnet 2 [1962–1983]. Fontfroide-le-Haut: Fata Morgana, 1998.

L'ajour. Paris: Poésie-Gallimard, 1998.

L'emportement du muet. Paris: Mercure de France, 2000.

Annotations sur l'espace non datées [Carnet 3]. Fontfroide-le-Haut: Fata Morgana, 2000.

Tumulte. Saint-Clément-la-Rivière: Fata Morgana, 2001.

Aveuglante ou banale: Essais sur la poésie, 1949–1959. Edited by Clément Layet. Paris: Le bruit du temps, 2011.

Une lampe dans la lumière aride: Carnets, 1949–1955. Edited by Clément Layet. Paris: Le bruit du temps, 2011.

Translations by André du Bouchet

William Faulkner. *Le gambit du cavalier.* Paris: Gallimard, 1951.

Shakespeare. *Périclès, Henri VIII, Les plaintes d'une amante,* et *Le phénix et la colombe.* In *Œuvres complètes,* Formes et Reflets. Paris: Le Club Français du Livre, 1961.

Joyce, James. *Finnegans Wake.* Fragments. Paris: Gallimard, 1962.

Shakespeare. *La Tempête.* Paris: Mercure de France, 1963.

Joyce, James. *Giacomo Joyce.* Paris: Gallimard, 1973.

Mandelstam, Ossip. *Voyage en Arménie.* Paris: Mercure de France, 1984.

Poèmes de Hölderlin. Paris: Mercure de France, 1986.

Poèmes de Paul Celan. Paris: Mercure de France, 1986.

Le méridien par Paul Celan. Saint-Clément: Fata Morgana, 1995.

Works by André du Bouchet Translated into English

The Uninhabited: Selected Poems of André du Bouchet. Translated by Paul Auster. New York: Living Hand, 1976. [Republished in *Translations/Paul Auster*. New York: Marsilio Publishers/EW Books, 1997.]

André du Bouchet: Where Heat Looms (Dans la chaleur vacante). Translated by David Mus, Los Angeles: Sun and Moon Classics, 2000.

Further Reading on André du Bouchet

Layet, Clément. *André du Bouchet*, Poètes d'aujourd'hui. Paris: Seghers, 2002.

L'Etrangère nos. 14–15 and 16–17–18. Double volume "André du Bouchet," texts compiled by François Rannou. Paris and Brussels: La lettre volée, June 2007.

Europe: Revue littéraire mensuelle, no. 986–987, "André du Bouchet." Paris: Centre National du Livre, June–July 2011.

NOTES ON SOURCES

This book is intended as an introductory reader, not a scholarly work. Basic information on sources is given below; for more complete references and further reading, consult the Select Bibliography. In the Introduction and elsewhere, I have translated a number of titles and quotations from the French. I render *Dans la chaleur vacante* as *In the Vacant Heat*, but compare the David Mus version listed above. For reasons stated on p. xxi, I prefer *Where the Sun* to *Or the Sun*, despite the heading given to the book by Gallimard. — HR

Introduction

xi   The epigraph by Herman Melville, from "The Conflict of Convictions" (1860–1861), is also the epigraph to du Bouchet's *Pourquoi si calmes* (1996).

xiii–   Biographical sources: Layet, ed., *André du Bouchet; L'Étran-*
xxviii   *gère*, double volume "André du Bouchet" (especially the "Chronologie" by Anne de Staël, 355–387, which includes numerous quotations from du Bouchet's letters and interviews with journalists); *Europe: Revue littéraire mensuelle*, "André du Bouchet" (particularly the interview with Paul Auster and the articles by Clément Layet, Victor Martinez, Didier Cahen, Antoine Emaz, Jean Bollack, and Michel Collot); conversations with Paul Auster, Yves Bonnefoy, and Sarah Plimpton, as well as my own recollections of André du Bouchet.

xxxiii   Giacometti's drawings and etchings: see the cover and frontispiece of this book.

xxxv–
xxxvi   On Willem de Kooning, see Mark Stevens and Annalyn Swan, *de Kooning: An American Master* (New York: Alfred A. Knopf, 2004).

xxxvi   Quotation from interview: see de Staël, "Chronologie."

xl   Royston quotation: see the preface to the *Cassandra* of Lycophron, in *The Remains of the Late Lord Viscount Royston . . .* (London: John Murray, 1838), 197.

xl   Remarks on Joyce: see "Lire Finnegans Wake?" the preface to du Bouchet's translations of excerpts from the work; republished in *Aveuglante ou banale* (2011), 116–117.

xli–xlii   References to Jourdan: see Pierre-Albert Jourdan, *The Straw Sandals: Selected Prose and Poetry*, translated by John Taylor (New York: Chelsea Editions, 2012).

xlii   Quotation from Paul Auster: see the Appendix.

Part One: Early Poems and Notebooks

"Air," unnumbered page inserted in *Air* (1951), reprinted in *Aveuglante ou banale* (2011), 64.

"I See Almost Nothing," from *Air* (1951), version from *Poèmes et proses* (1995), 9.

"Alphabet Fire," "Leaves of Day," "Room," "Term," poems from *Air* (1951) and *Air: 1950–1953* (1977), unpublished selection courtesy of Clément Layet.

"The piercing thorns . . . ," from a notebook dated 1951, pages transcribed by the author, published in *Aveuglante ou banale* (2011), 133–135.

Pages
18–89:   excerpts from notebooks dated 1953–1955, published in *Une lampe dans la lumière aride* (2011), 189–327.

Part Two: *The Uninhabited*

"From the Edge of the Scythe," "Lapse," "Meteor," "Accidents," "The White Motor," "What the Lamp Burned," and "Giving Over" from *Dans la chaleur vacante* (1961), 9–11, 23, 36, 40, 57–72, 74–76, 105.

"Where the Sun," "The Uninhabited," "Marking Posts," "Plain," "Postponement," "The Light of the Blade," "This Surface," and "Plow-Ridge," from *Où le soleil* (1968), np.

Part Three: Late Poems

"Painting," from *Ici en deux* (1986), version from *Poèmes et proses* (1995), 41–42.

"I Interletter . . . ," from *L'incohérence* (1979), version from *Poèmes et proses* (1995), 50–52.

"Bygone" and "Flash of Light," from *Laisses* (1979), versions from *Poèmes et proses* (1995), 64–69.

"Withdrawn from a Future," from *Axiales* (1992), 63–65.

"Crete," "Stone or Water," "Swiftness," and "Blood," from *Axiomes* (in *Ici en deux*) (1986), np.

"Painting," from *Retours sur le vent* (1995), version from *Poèmes et proses* (1995), 195–97.

"From a Notebook," from *Pourquoi si calmes* (1996), 45–51.

BIOGRAPHIES

André du Bouchet, born in 1924, is widely acknowledged as one of the greatest French poets of the twentieth century. Among many other honors, he received the National Poetry Prize of France in 1983.

His family fled wartorn Europe to the United States in 1941. He studied literature at Amherst and Harvard and returned to France in 1948. In 1961 he published *Dans la chaleur vacante* (*In the Vacant Heat*), a poetry collection that brought him to the forefront of international letters. This was followed by *Où le soleil* (*Where the Sun*) in 1968, a cycle of poems that further sealed his reputation.

In the late sixties he edited the influential literary and artistic journal *L'Éphémère* along with Yves Bonnefoy, Jacques Dupin, and Paul Celan. A versatile translator, he produced French versions of Shakespeare, Hölderlin, Joyce, Mandelstam, and Pasternak. He was a prolific essayist on contemporary art, the author of seminal studies of Giacometti in 1972 and 1991. He collaborated on books with Pierre Tal Coat, Bram van Velde, and many other artists.

In the seventies, eighties, and nineties, he published a steady stream of innovative poetry. He assembled selections from his notebooks as well as anthologies drawn from his previous work. Until his death in 2001, André du Bouchet spent many months each year in the mountains of the Drôme.

Paul Auster is known worldwide for his novels, which have won him numerous awards, as well as for his films, memoirs, essays, and poetry. But he is also an authority on French literature and a noted translator from the French. In 1982 he edited *The Random House*

Book of Twentieth-Century French Poetry, and he has published translations of Joubert, Mallarmé, Sartre, Blanchot, Dupin, and many other authors. His translations of du Bouchet date from the years 1967–1971; they were first published in book form by Living Hand in 1976. He has revised them for this edition. Paul Auster lives in Brooklyn with his wife, the writer Siri Hustvedt.

Hoyt Rogers has published his poems, stories, essays, and translations in many books and periodicals. He translates from the French, German, Italian, and Spanish. His translations of Jorge Luis Borges were included in the Viking-Penguin centenary edition of 1999. Farrar, Straus and Giroux published his translation of Yves Bonnefoy's *The Curved Planks* in 2006, and his anthology of the poet's recent work, *Second Simplicity*, appeared in the Margellos Series at Yale in 2012. In 2014 his translation of Bonnefoy's *The Digamma* was published by Seagull Books. Hoyt Rogers divides his time between the Dominican Republic and Italy.